Are You Sustainable?

THE FUTURE OF WORK

Are You Sustainable?

MORTEN STRANGE

Marshall Cavendish
Business

Published in 2023 by Marshall Cavendish Business
An imprint of Marshall Cavendish International

A member of the
Times Publishing Group

Other Marshall Cavendish Offices:
Marshall Cavendish Corporation, 800 Westchester Ave, Suite N-641, Rye Brook, NY 10573, USA • Marshall Cavendish International (Thailand) Co Ltd, 253 Asoke, 16th Floor, Sukhumvit 21 Road, Klongtoey Nua, Wattana, Bangkok 10110, Thailand • Marshall Cavendish (Malaysia) Sdn Bhd, Times Subang, Lot 46, Subang Hi-Tech Industrial Park, Batu Tiga, 40000 Shah Alam, Selangor Darul Ehsan, Malaysia

Marshall Cavendish is a registered trademark of Times Publishing Limited

National Library Board, Singapore Cataloguing in Publication Data
Name(s): Strange, Morten.
Title: Are you sustainable? / Morten Strange.
Other Title(s): Future of work.
Description: Singapore : Marshall Cavendish Business, 2023.
Identifier(s): ISBN 978-981-5113-53-2 (paperback)
Subject(s): LCSH: Finance, Personal--Moral and ethical aspects. | Investments--Moral and ethical aspects.
Classification: DDC 332.024--dc2

Printed in Singapore

Contents

WELCOME TO THE FUTURE OF WORK

Are your investments sustainable? Is your lifestyle sustainable? Are *you* sustainable? As we enter an age filled with environmental, financial and political uncertainties, the key to survival will be the ability to future-proof our personal livelihoods, our communities and our ecosystems.

This prescient and practical book explores the myriad choices that we make as workers, consumers, investors, citizens and human beings. It offers not only a deep dive into how the world has come to be this way, but also guides you on how to navigate the sometimes ethically complex dilemmas of building financial independence in the face of job insecurity, rampant inflation and environmental destruction.

The Future of Work is a game-changing collection of business books that explore the rapidly evolving landscape of work today. Within the next five years, many jobs will disappear, many will be created, but what is certain is that all will change. The titles in this new series, written by some of the most influential business leaders, thought leaders, practitioners and consultants in the industry, cover everything from business trends and technological innovations, to revolutions in work culture and the critical skills you'll need in order to stay ahead of the curve.

Preface

As a follow-up to my *Be Financially Free: How to become salary independent in today's economy*, Marshall Cavendish approached me in 2018 and encouraged me to write a book which we ended up calling *The Ethical Investor's Handbook: How to grow your money without wrecking the earth*. In it, we try to establish what is wrong with the world and how investors can navigate the investment landscape while applying their ethical values at the same time. In all my books, I try to give practical, pragmatic advice to readers in the "how to" spirit. I do that because I myself am a reader; I read other writers' work and although I find value in technical textbooks, I also appreciate it when the author occasionally inserts some useful real-life case stories into his arguments; so I try to do that myself.

In the beginning of 2023, the publishing team from Marshall Cavendish approached me again and proposed that I should write a volume in their new series, The Future of Work. I was keen to explore the sustainability phenomenon in general, to try to unwrap a concept that has become something of a craze in the current economic, financial, social and political debate. So in this volume, we focus on the sustainably issue in all its forms, although economic and financial sustainability of course feature highly. In my view, economics is the foundation for most other things that happen in society, and financial wellbeing and freedom is a condition and a prerequisite for all other types of freedom. You cannot be really free if you are forced to work for a boss you don't respect, in a job you don't enjoy, just to make ends meet from paycheck to paycheck. That is no life. Only savings and financial resources can give you the power to quit, change your life, move if you need to, do what you love to do with the people you like, live the life you dream of.

But sustainability is more than just a bit of money in the bank. To be truly sustainable, you have to live in harmony with your surroundings and in equilibrium with the environment. You can eat into the environmental cake while enriching yourself for only so long – there are limits and boundaries as to how far the exploitation can go. So in this volume we will cover other aspects of sustainability as well. To show just how close to home these issues are, I will make use of many real-life case stories, including some from my own experience.

Let me clarify one thing right away: I am not the perfect role model for sustainability! I have kids, I drive a car, I travel overseas, I eat meat – according to all surveys, those are the four major environmental sins, in that order of "badness"; I will go into this in more detail in the book. I even worked in the oil and gas industry for 10 years. In other words, I am personally in no position to point fingers and shame anyone regarding their environmental footprint, so I try not to.

One thing I did do right though, throughout my brief professional career, was that instead of squandering the money I made from extraction work on conspicuous consumption and point-less consumer stuff, I saved the financial capital I generated and made it grow, so that I could work less. For what it is worth, I encourage my friends and my readers to aim to do the same. I try to support this strategy with proof, exploring the various sources available, while keeping an open mind to opposing interpretations and points of view. I am not an academic, but I have worked with numbers all my life in engineering and finance and I value what the precise evidence out there tells us.

In the five years since *The Ethical Investor's Handbook* came out, we have lived through plenty of remarkable and startling events. The Trump presidency uprooted much of the Washington establishment, and Trump's campaign against "free trade" contributed to the deglobalization movement. In the meantime, the humanitarian crises in Syria, Yemen, Venezuela as well as much of Africa, Central America and South Asia created a record flow of illegal migrants seeking to get into the United States, as well as the EU, even if that bloc was weakened in 2019 by Brexit. Climate change issues have caught on in the public debate since 2017 – somewhat like a wildfire in California; then in 2020 we had the Covid-19 pandemic and in 2022 a major hot war in the heart of Europe, with the threat of nuclear escalation looming large over humanity once again.

In fact, one of the trendiest words of our time seems to be "unprecedented". The refugee crisis, the Coronavirus epidemic, the floods, the droughts, the wildfires ... they have all at one time or another been described as unprecedented by the media, which hardly indicates a business-as-usual era.

So there we are. Let us try to find out, in the midst of all this, *are you sustainable?*

Morten Strange
Singapore
August 2023

1
The Future Is Now

THERE IS NO PRESENT

People who study time point out that apart from in grammatical use, there is really no present tense; there is only the future. As soon as the future arrives, it becomes the past. It might seem a trivial observation, but personally I have found it useful to think of time this way. Especially as you get older, you spend more time reflecting on the past, so for young people it is important to appreciate that to have a good past you must plan the future well. In other words, you should make sure that you plan your life ahead, such that it will be filled with interesting events that you can later reflect back on with joy.

Although you can learn to live with your past, it will never go away; good and bad memories are stored in equal measure. In Clint Eastwood's excellent movie about the Battle of Iwo Jima in World War II, *Flags of Our Fathers*, one of the characters suddenly on his deathbed many years later becomes obsessed with what happened to one of his friends during fighting on that Pacific island and calls out repeatedly: "Where is Iggy?" Things you thought you had forgotten, or at least put behind you, are still there. So take steps to plan for good events going forward, so that you will have a good set of memories to look back on later.

In other words, since there is no "now", the future is really the only present we have to live in.

PREDICTING THE FUTURE

"It is difficult to make predictions, especially about the future" – several sources take credit for this quote, but no matter who said it first, it is true. Francis Fukuyama tried that, to predict the future, and he failed miserably. His belief was that with the end of the Cold War in 1989–91, we would see "the end of history" (the title of his 1992 book), with Western liberal democratic values taking over and the mixed market economy and financial globalization accepted uniformly everywhere.

Although Fukuyama is a self-confessed neo-conservative, in this regard he has much in common with Karl Marx. To both of them, human history is seen as a linear progression leading forward to an end development stage, the so-called "end of history"; sooner or later all peoples in the world will aspire to this goal and all countries will end here. In Marx's case, this final social order was communism, where a classless society of workers would own the means of production. In Fukuyama's case ... well, the social order would be like the Western countries of his period, some 30 years ago. Of course, as it turned out, none of these societal models were universally adopted by everyone. Communism certainly didn't work, and those countries that tried it stagnated and failed. Even the wonderful liberal democracy that Fukuyama championed didn't really fit all countries.

When I grew up in Europe in the 1950s and 60s, we didn't learn much about China. Except we kids were told that we should finish our dinner because "there are starving children in China who would love to have your food"! I ended up working on and off in China from 1982 to 1986, sometimes for weeks and months at a time, and that was a real eye-opening experience. Much later, in this century, when I got married to an ethnic Chinese, I decided to check out Chinese history to try and better understand where these people were coming from. Among the things I learnt was that the Chinese traditionally do not view history, like Fukuyama and Marx did, as a continuous forward progression with a final, pretty much inevitable, end goal of socioeconomic development. The Chinese might see history more as an oscillating sequence of episodes, going from chaos to order and back to chaos again. This is how much of their – very long – civilization has played out in the past, and the Chinese have no reason to believe that it will not continue in the future. At the moment, post the disorderly Mao Zedong era and after Deng Xiaoping and now Xi Jinping took over, the country is in a state of order. But somehow I suspect that many Chinese do not believe that this stage is permanent; chaos could erupt again at any moment.

A CASE STORY FROM RECENT HISTORY

After the fall of the Berlin Wall and the disintegration of the Soviet Union, we did indeed seem to have a pretty harmonious period.

I remember those years well. I had my twin boys born in 1988 and another boy in 1991. The 1990s were a decade where there was a vision of a Europe "from Lisbon to Vladivostok", as Eastern Europe as well as Russia and China opened up for trade and investments. In Singapore, Prime Minister Goh Chok Tong signed some 15 Free Trade Agreements during his tenure (1992–2004), including an important one with the US.[1] Globally, the personal computer revolution resulted in tremendous increase in productivity, and in the US, President Bill Clinton managed to reduce the government debt-to-GDP ratio by collecting more taxes and reducing military spending, from 41% in 1990 to 33% in 2000 (at the end of 2022 it was 123%!).[2] In Southeast Asia, important democratic reforms were initiated in the Philippines, Thailand and Indonesia. For a while it did indeed appear as if the prediction of Fukuyama and his friends was valid.

But it wasn't to last. The Western intellectuals and politicians became so convinced about their invincibility that they went as far as trying to reshape those countries that still didn't subscribe to their worldview. Personally I believe that is where they went wrong. This policy of forced regime change started with the NATO bombing of Serbia in 1999 and continued this century with interventionist wars in Afghanistan (2001), Iraq (2003), Syria (2011) and Libya (2011); you could add various conflicts with Western involvement in Yemen and Africa to this list too.

It seems that the people of the world don't like to be told what to do. During the last century, they rejected Marx's communism, and now in this one, many reject the neo-con/liberal socialist order championed by most NATO and EU countries. As it turns out, one size doesn't fit all; that goes for shoes as well as socioeconomic models. In spite of Fukuyama's predictions, today, 30 years after his book came out, only a small minority of people live in a society that he would condone. In 2022, Fukuyama's soulmates at the Economist Intelligence Unit (EIU) came out with a report entitled "Frontline Democracy and the Battle for Ukraine".[3] The report was a special edition of the *Democracy Index* published annually by this think-tank. According to this report, only 24 countries in the world live in so-called "full" democracies; they constitute 14% of all countries surveyed and just 8% of the world population. Of course, the UK, where the EIU is based, is one of those, a "full" democracy! Another 48 countries are "flawed" democracies, 36 are "hybrid" regimes, and 59 are outright "authoritarian" regimes. Notice that governments which the EIU does not like are now called regimes.

If you read between the lines of a report like this, it might become clearer why most people in the world do not sign up for the NATO and EU-based liberal-socialist world order. The main point of the 2022 edition is that we should all rally around the Kiev-based Ukraine government fighting for freedom and democracy. That government came to power after the violent Maidan coup in 2014 overthrew the elected government of Viktor Yanukovych and chased the president into exile. The coup leaders then started a civil war against the Russian-speaking minority living in the east of Ukraine, which led to a de facto partition of the country. With opposition parties dissolved and critical media banned, the freedom-loving Ukrainian nationalists started preparing the armed forces for a decisive push to drive all ethnic minorities out of the country, assisted by their backers in NATO and the EU. The Minsk peace agreements of 2014 and 2015 only served as a cover to stall for time while Ukraine built up their armed forces, as Angela Merkel and Francois Hollande, who co-signed in the Minsk II agreement, both later admitted.[4] In 2022, Russia finally intervened militarily to defend their people and protect Russia itself from further NATO aggression.

The 2022 EIU report acknowledges that a vast majority of the world population lives in countries that do *not* support NATO and EU's sanctions against Russia or their armed support for the Kiev nationalists. According to the report, only 16.1% of the world population live in countries that condemn Russia, although if you look at these countries' share of the world gross domestic product (GDP), this is much higher, at 61.2%.

Most countries in Asia refused to condemn Russia for the February 2022 invasion of Ukraine; Singapore was the only country in Southeast Asia to do so. Law and Home Affairs Minister K. Shanmugam explained that for Singapore, this was not about being pro- or anti-Russian or pro- or anti- any other country, it was about following the rules of international law and respecting the territorial integrity of all countries, just as Singapore on previous occasions had protested against armed invasions of Cambodia by Vietnam (1978) and Grenada by the US (1983). He added that the Western narrative of the conflict "doesn't convey the whole picture. It too conveniently absolves the West of any responsibility for the way the events have unfolded."[5]

He then explained that Russia has legitimate security concerns, drawing parallels to the Cuban Missile Crisis in 1962, when the US objected to having Soviet missiles stationed near their borders, forcing the Soviet Union – with the threat of nuclear war – to eventually back down. "The West has to reflect on whether

Russia's concerns were adequately dealt with," he said. "Otherwise, it will look like double standards are being applied."

I can only agree. I have seen many bears over the years, of three different species. I have hiked and camped alone in Grizzly Bear country, and I never had any problems with them. The secret is to leave the bears alone. Give them some space. They live in the hills and you have to respect that. The Russian bear is no different.

When I see the Ukrainian president travel the world, treated like a rock star everywhere he goes, I have to ask myself: Is he the role model for successful national development that we should aspire to? What did he and his government do to respect and protect and assist all ethnic minorities in Ukraine – Russian, Romanian, Bulgarian and Polish alike? What did he do to foster friendly ties between all nations, big and small, to develop international peaceful cooperation of trade and investments, to build a prosperous and unified country? Did he build up financial and social reserves, so that he could weather a downturn and help others in need?

In Singapore we do all that. It can be done. Like Ukraine, we have various ethnic minorities, different religious and linguistic groups. But we don't outlaw their languages, ban their religions, bombard their living areas. In fact, we have affirmative action programmes to help minorities and disadvantaged social groups develop and catch up. In Singapore, we go to great lengths to get along with everyone in the world, including our much bigger – and sometimes a bit difficult – neighbours. This is not rocket science; this is just ordinary decency and common sense.

Personally I think that it is this diversity of peoples and cultures that gives meaning to humanity. Just like we should protect the biodiversity of life, with its many different life forms and species, each playing a part in the ecological landscape, we should also maintain the diversity of cultures and languages and we should do everything we can to maintain social harmony and peace between different groups of people and different nations. Bilateral relations and regional economic cooperation zones are the way forward, not military blocs confronting and threatening each other.

From a sustainability point of view, war is not sustainable and should be avoided at all costs. We should reduce our spending on arms and wars, not expand it. The combined military spending of NATO countries was $1,190 billion in 2022; the number has been going up every year since 2014, in spite of our concern about financial instability and resources depletion.[6] By comparison, Russia spent $66 billion on defence in 2021, down from $88 billion in 2013; presumably this number will go up as well when the 2022 numbers are in. As a matter of interest, China spent $293 billion on defence in 2021, according to the same source, statista.com.

If people really cannot get along, they should meet up and decide on a partition, preferably amicably. Just like married couples do, if the union doesn't work out as planned. Since World War II, divorce between nations has happened time and again, sometimes peacefully, sometimes not quite so, but always with a better outcome for everyone in the long run than war. The Partition of India in 1947 was tough for many at the time; the peace-loving Mahatma Gandhi for one was devastated that his peoples couldn't get along. East and West Pakistan even split up further much later in 1971, in what became known as the Bangladesh Liberation War. That was the year I graduated from the social sciences stream in high school, and we followed this conflict closely. On the Indian subcontinent, it was all bloody and traumatic at the time, but looking back now, in the end a divorce was inevitable; a reunification today is out of the question.

In more recent times, Czechoslovakia, Yugoslavia, Sudan split up, Eritrea, East Timor and Kosovo gained independence. What is so wrong with the Russian-speaking part of Ukraine breaking off? They are obviously not welcomed by the EU-supporters in the east of the country, so just let the Russia-supporters go. Nothing is worth fighting a war over; it is simply too costly in terms of finances, environmental damage and sheer human suffering.

Even if we cannot quite agree on how to interpret the events in Ukraine from 2014 and onwards, I think that we can all agree that the world we have today is not really the world that many of us envisaged in 1992. The unipolar world order in the making at that time didn't develop quite according to plan; today we have to deal with a multipolar world community trying to grapple with difficult issues.

SO, WHAT *WILL* THE FUTURE LOOK LIKE?

We have seen that it is difficult to make predictions, especially about the future. But that hasn't stopped lots of people from trying, academic researchers as well as creative writers. In the latter camp, I always like a good futuristic show and there are plenty of them. Just take your pick and see if any of the visions match your expectations or taste.

My personal favourite is *Soylent Green* from 1973, a special year for me because I dropped out of college that summer and started working for a living, one of the best decisions I ever made. In this movie, it is year 2022(!) and American society has degraded into chronic overpopulation and catastrophic environmental collapse; 40 million people are cramped into New York City where most sleep rough on the streets while a few live in luxurious gated communities. The state offers assisted suicide to deal with the overpopulation, and the main source of food for the masses is a protein bar made from marine algae called Soylent Green. Sounds familiar ... somewhat, right? But it gets better: Hollywood tough-guy Charlton Heston plays a police officer who while investigating a murder in the rich part of town stumbles on information that the environment outside of the city has deteriorated further and can no longer sustain soylent production. So he follows the garbage trucks carrying crushed protesters and suicide cadavers to a disposal plant, where, it turns out, the dead bodies are being processed into food for humans. The movie ends as Heston's character, wounded after a gunfight at the plant, shouts: "Soylent green is PEOPLE!"

The theme rings true with this statement made by Ted Turner during an interview some years back: "It will be 8 degrees hotter in 30 to 40 years, and basically none of the crops will grow, most of the people left will have died and the rest of us will live like cannibals ... living conditions will be intolerable."

But then, as you know, for each point of view there is another one, looking from a different angle in the opposite direction; this is very much true for artistic expressions of future scenarios. For the rose-coloured-glasses crowd, there is *Tomorrowland*, a 2015 sci-fi flick by Walt Disney Pictures. In this one, George Clooney plays a misunderstood genius scientist who together with an enthusiastic young tech-lover girl defeats the nasty environmental doomsday preachers, who actually turn out to be the bad guys. In this movie, the environmentalists not only predict an apocalyptic future for mankind, they actively aim to make it happen – to punish humanity for mismanaging the Earth. But of course, Clooney's character saves the day, and a future with a beautiful Earth, optimistic young people and unlimited space travel to other galaxies is ensured.

My take on the future? Funny you should ask; one of my sons (Daniel, a millennial, born 1988, living in Cyprus) asked me exactly that question last time he was out visiting us in Singapore. It forced me to put into words what is somewhat difficult to articulate, because, in a way, your idea of the future is somewhat of an emotional notion. You can only envisage the future by extrapolating from what you've experienced. I consider myself a "pragmatic pessimist" (I will expand on this term in Chapter 7). Like Ted Turner, quoted above, I think that times ahead will be hard for most people. I think that humanity is reaching some limits for what the Earth can comfortably provide for us. I believe that as we come to these limits, there will be less for everyone – mainly in terms of space, but also in terms of energy, minerals and quality food. We can still get the stuff we need, but it will be more and more expensive to extract, so productivity will decline. This will manifest in higher real prices and a situation of "peak prosperity", a concept introduced by Chris Martenson, who wrote *Prosper!* (2015); and technology will not be able to save us. In my view, this process has already started and will get amplified going forward; that is what I mean by the title of this chapter. Development will be more uneven, a retreating tide will tend to strand all boats, but in some countries, and some regions within countries, some boats will be more stranded than others. People will migrate from the bad places to the slightly less bad; they are already doing so. The ecological breakdown, the financial constrictions, the discontent ... going forward it will be a train wreck in slow motion, but it could get accelerated if social unrest and wars break out.

But I also told my son, and I tell everyone else who cares to listen, that the world is a miraculous and beautiful place. It doesn't matter if we have to do with a little less physical stuff in the future; we have enough already. Live a simple life. Some of my best meals have been not in five-star hotel fine-dining restaurants but sitting with my wife – or alone for that matter – outside the tent at a campfire off the trail in the hills, cooking freeze-dried soup and instant noodles. Is a storm coming this way? Maybe, bring it on; who says life should be easy? When the going gets tough, the tough get going. We will prevail.

AND THEN THERE IS THE ENVIRONMENT

I was telling a family friend the other day that I was working on a new book about sustainability, and she asked me: "What kind of sustainability? What do you mean by that?" I was a bit taken aback. I presumed that everyone would recognize what the concept of sustainability relates to, but you cannot take that for granted. So, we have to keep in mind that there are many types of sustainability, and we may not necessarily all be talking about the same thing when someone brings up the term.

Judging from my experience, and from the public debate, sustainability falls into two broad categories. In the next chapter, and throughout much of the rest of the book, we will deal in more detail with the economic factor of this equation: How will the macroeconomic situation impact our future and our prospects for financial and material sustainability in general, and how, more specifically, can you position yourself to be financially resilient. But you cannot have a book about sustainability and not bring in the environment; for many people this would be the key element of sustainability, i.e. stable and successfully maintained and continued development going forward.

Environmental sustainability is covered in other books, *many* other books in fact. In addition, in my book *Be Financially Free*, I deal with environmental degradation and resource limitations in the chapter, "It's a Finite World". In *The Ethical Investor's Handbook*, I expand this analysis throughout the book. However, five years have gone by since that last book came out, and with regard to sustainability, things move astonishingly fast. Virtually every single day we hear news about either (1) a weather-related event such as a hurricane, typhoon, cyclone, tornado or bushfire wreaking havoc somewhere, or (2) a new study showing the decline of mammals, birds, insects, fishes, forest cover or arable land, or even (3) human suffering caused by displacement, illegal immigration, hunger, water scarcity, droughts or floods. And in every single story, the commentator will point out the culprit, the reason for all this destruction and misery: climate change, global warming caused by unsustainable development. The message is always the same: We have to change our ways. And the result is also always the same: We don't.

We have been warned about our unsustainable ways for decades. But now the future is here. *The Limits to Growth* – the best-selling ecology book of all time, first published in 1972 and updated in 2004 – identified 2030 as the year when serious repercussions from unsustainable economic growth would start to be felt by mankind. And as many of us expected, it is only really when houses burn and people drown that the general public pays any attention; and that is exactly what it has come down to.

You could ask yourself: How have climate change, global warming, resource scarcity and pollution – the by-products of economic growth – changed life for *you*? In today's future world, I know of many people in various countries who are paying the price for prosperity. Friends in Alaska with sink-holes on their property due to the melting of permafrost, the neighbour's house collapsing and completely worthless. Friends in Europe lament the loss of common birds and insects and amphibians, with trees dying from diseases and pests made worse by the warm winters. Our friends in northern Thailand suffer horrific air pollution from vehicular exhaust fumes and bush-fires every dry season. In Malaysia, the floods and landslides are getting worse every year due to increase in rainfall, forest clearance and rivers clogged up with garbage.

Here in safe and well-managed Singapore, surrounded by a favourable geography that shields us from typhoons and earth tremors, we are better off than most; but even here I hear older people complaining about the weather being hotter than they ever remember. This is confirmed by statistics: from 1980 to 2020, the annual mean temperature increased from 26.9 to 28.0°C. And it is only going to get worse from here. By the end of the century, the long-term effects of climate change are projected to lead to a temperature increase of 1.4–4.6°C and a rise in sea level by up to 1 metre.[7]

If you think that a 1.1°C increase in average air temperature is a problem, what will +4.6°C be like? We don't know, and personally I don't expect to be around to find out; but either way, weather-related events and associated concerns are likely to increase in frequency and severity, so it is something that young people of today will have to factor into their planning.

WHAT ARE WE DOING ABOUT IT THEN?

Very little. Just look at a few of those surveys and reports published during the short time that has passed since my last book came out. For one thing, loss of tropical rainforests, critical for global climate stability and biodiversity, has accelerated, not slowed down. Why? Right, you guessed it: "Despite the commitment of hundreds of companies to get deforestation out of their supply chains by 2020, vast areas continue to be cleared for soy, beef, palm oil and other commodities," the World Resources Institute reported. "In the cases of soy and palm oil, global demand is artificially inflated by policies that incentivize using food as a feedstock for biofuels."[8] The good old economic-growth mantra is at play again; some politics and sheer mismanagement also chip in. While some $1 billion is allocated yearly from developed countries to pay poorer countries to protect their forests, over

$100 billion is provided "for financing agriculture and other land sector investments that put forests at risk". Not to worry, we will just have another conference about this. The very week in 2018 that these figures were reported, "more than 500 citizens of Forestry World are gathering at the Oslo Tropical Forest Forum to reflect on the last 10 years of efforts to protect forests, and chart a way forward". As usual: We will all meet again next year, and then we will chart a way forward!

What about CO_2 (carbon dioxide) emissions? At the 2021 UN Climate Change Conference COP26, US President Joe Biden promised that his government would subsidize "clean energy" to mitigate the "climate crisis": "We will cut US greenhouse gas emissions by well over 1 gigaton by 2030."[9] The very next day, back home in Washington, D.C., he lamented that high oil and gasoline prices were "a consequence of, thus far, the refusal of Russia or the OPEC nations to pump more oil".[10] Later on in his presidency, Biden ordered more crude oil to come on the market by drawing down the Strategic Petroleum Reserve and authorizing more exploration and production in the so-called Willow project in Arctic Alaska. About that latter decision, Athan Manuel, director of the Sierra Club's lands protection programme, said: "No proposal poses a bigger threat to lands, wildlife, communities and our climate ... Oil and gas leasing on public lands and waters must end – full stop. The eyes of the world are watching to see whether this administration will live up to its climate promises."[11] So will it live up to its climate promises? I think that question has already been answered.

Another issue: Land use – is it getting better? It doesn't really seem so. According to the think-tank IPPR in 2019, "human impacts have reached a critical stage and threaten to destabilize society and the global economy. Scientists warn of a potentially deadly combination of factors. These include climate change, mass loss of species, topsoil erosion, forest felling and acidifying oceans."[12] Specifically about soil erosion, the BBC report summarized that "topsoil is being lost 10 to 40 times faster than it is being replenished by natural processes. Since the mid-20th century, 30% of the world's arable land has become unproductive due to erosion." It concluded on an ominous note: "The IPPR says many scientists believe we have entered a new era of rapid environmental change ... 'We define this as the age of environmental breakdown to better highlight the severity of the scale, pace and implications of environmental destabilisation resulting from aggregate human activity.'"

The age of environmental breakdown ... this is not really a good era to be in; most people call it the Anthropocene (I will get back to this term in Chapter 6). But I do sympathize with people who are a bit tired of hearing about all this, our environmental calamities. Even I – and I am concerned about the state of our environment – am somewhat put off when I hear Al Gore rant about nuclear bombs going off. In a clip from an interview during the 2023 World Economic Forum, repeated night after night on Bloomberg financial TV, Gore gets a little carried away: "We're still putting 162 million tons [of CO_2] into [the atmosphere] every single day, and the accumulated amount is now trapping as much extra heat as would be released by 600,000 Hiroshima-class atomic bombs exploding every single day on the earth. That's what's boiling the oceans, creating these atmospheric rivers and rain bombs, and sucking the moisture out of the land and creating the droughts and melting the ice and raising the sea level and causing these waves of climate refugees, predicted to reach one billion in this century."[13] 600,000 nuclear bombs every day? When you hear this kind of scare-mongering ad nauseam, I think most people's eyes simply glaze over and they go back to checking the latest online car catalogues: Should I buy the new 4.0L V8 SUV or make do with the 3.0L V6? Especially when outrageous statements like these are made by someone who just took some $100 million from the sale of his TV station to the oil-rich Qatar government.[14]

But whichever way they are presented or dealt with, the environmental problems we face are dire, and we have to consider them. So before we move on to the economic aspects of the sustainability issue, I will let millennial American journalist David Wallace-Wells get the last word in on the environmental angle. Wallace-Wells wrote *The Uninhabitable Earth* (2020); in different chapters of the book, he lists the "elements of chaos" that we are facing, and they are the usual suspects: global warming, flooding, wildfires, pandemics, dying oceans, unbreathable air, food and water scarcity, economic collapse, and finally, climate conflict. Studying a list like this will really make your day, right? Wallace-Wells also, rightly in my view, points out that by now we all basically know about the problems. And yet we do nothing. He says: "More than half the carbon exhaled into the atmosphere by the burning of fossil fuels has been emitted in just the past three decades... This means that we have now done as much damage to the environment knowingly as we ever managed in ignorance."

Even the Covid-19 pandemic, which ground our global economic activity to a near-halt, could put only a small dent in our annual CO_2 emissions.

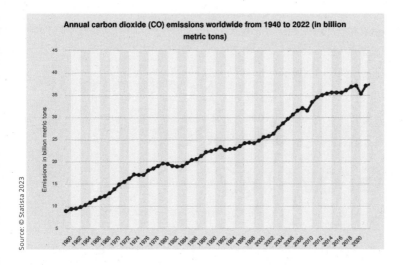

Annual carbon dioxide (CO) emissions worldwide from 1940 to 2022 (in billion metric tons)

Source: © Statista 2023

After a small dip during the pandemic, emissions are right back growing again. In terms of CO_2 concentrations in the atmosphere, they even increased during the Covid years, from 411 parts per million (ppm) in 2019 to 416 ppm in 2021 and then 418 ppm in 2022.[15] That's the highest concentration seen throughout the Pleistocene (going back 2.6 million years) as well as the Holocene (which followed 11,700 years ago), where the highest CO_2 concentration was 280 ppm and the world was generally a much colder place; atmospheric concentrations of CH_4 (methane) were significantly lower too (Angus, 2016). There is no stopping us, is there?

Personally I am not too obsessed with CO_2 and CH_4 emissions alone; they are just two indicators out of many, and their consequences are not fully understood. What I read out of numbers like these, however, is that there is a huge disconnect between all the sustainability jargon by journalists, writers, influencers, decision-makers, corporate bigwigs and public leaders, and the reality on the ground – and in the air. In the next chapter, we will look at what this means for our economy.

31

2

The New Economy: Can We Keep Growing?

SOME MORE PREDICTIONS

Nowhere are predictions more prevalent than within the sphere of economics and finance. Especially in the subsection of finance that deals with capital allocation and investments, future predictions are everything. I have been to countless investment seminars and meetings and the theme almost always boils down to: Will the markets go up or down tomorrow? Should I buy or sell? What does the future hold?

I have a securities trading account with SAXO Bank and every year in December, the bank sends out a newsletter to its customers with its forecast for the following calendar year. I used to keep those on file and look at them a year later, but I don't do that anymore, it was really a waste of my time. The last edition of *SAXO's*

Outrageous Predictions I have is dated December 2018, covering the year 2019. That year, 2019, SAXO predicted that "Trump tells Powell 'You're fired'", "Prime Minister Corbyn sends GBP/USD to parity", "Corporate credit crunch pushes Netflix into GE's vortex", "Germany enters recession", "X-class solar flare creates chaos and inflicts $2 trillion of damage", "Global transportation tax enacted as climate panic spreads", "IMF and World Bank announce intend to stop measuring GDP". I will not go into detail about what all this means; I just want to establish than none of this nonsense happened in 2019, or in any of the following years: Germany's GDP grew 1.1% in 2019, Netflix's share price rose from $339 to $345 during the year, and peaked at $690 in 2021. Jerome Powell is still (2023) in charge of the Federal Reserve, and Jeremy Corbyn never became Prime Minister of the UK.

The world of economics and finance is full of talking heads making predictions that never come true. In *Be Financially Free*, I discussed a 2007 survey of 36 American financial analysts, in which 35 of these top economic experts predicted a period of slow growth for the following year, 2008. What happened instead was of course the worst financial crisis the country had seen since 1929. The US and much of the rest of the world dropped into a recession, and 8 million Americans lost their jobs. Only one analyst out of 36 predicted economic contraction for the coming year and got it right!

Or what about this howler from Janet Yellen back in 2017, when she was still Chair of the US Federal Reserve, the central bank of the largest economy in the world? "Would I say there will never, ever be another financial crisis? You know probably that would be going too far but I do think we're much safer and I hope that it will not be in our lifetimes and I don't believe it will be."[16] So the media ran with this conclusion in the summary: "U.S. Federal Reserve Chair Janet Yellen said on Tuesday that she does not believe that there will be another financial crisis for at least as long as she lives, thanks largely to reforms of the banking system since the 2007-09 crash."

In my view, that is a catastrophically casual and irresponsible declaration from one of the most influential people in the world. Yellen lost her job at the Federal Reserve the following year, but her complete failure in assessing financial risk didn't stop her from getting another top job later. Shortly after Joe Biden was inaugurated as President in January 2021, he appointed Yellen as his Secretary of the Treasury, i.e. finance minister.

LET'S LOOK AT SOME OF THE RISKS

All right, in all fairness to Dr Yellen, some financial headwinds are hard to predict. The year after she lost her job at the Federal Reserve, towards the end of 2019, a mysterious flu virus emerged from the Chinese city of Wuhan; who could have seen that coming? The next year and into 2022, much of the world came to a standstill; this was a so-called Black Swan event, an unknown unknown, as Donald Rumsfeld would have said.[17] The Black Swan reference originates from old Europe, where it was presumed that all swans were white; and they were for centuries, until black swans (*Cygnus atratus*) were found in Australia. So in finance, a Black Swan event has come to symbolize a high-impact episode that is next to impossible to predict.

Covid-19 had a massive global impact on social as well as financial conditions; it pushed economies worldwide into more debt and millions of people into poverty. We will get back to this a bit later. But claiming that the incident was completely impossible to foresee would not be entirely correct. We have had warnings about serious outbreaks of pandemics for as long as I can remember, mainly about highly infectious and hard-to-treat viruses. One of my favourite writers is Desmond Morris; I read his *Naked Ape* when it came out in 1967 and most of his other books after that. Dr Morris warned the world repeatedly about the possibility of a deadly virus outbreak throughout much of his life. More recently, David Quammen wrote *Spillover: Animal Infections and the Next Pandemic* (2012). In this meticulously researched work, Quammen explains the origins and consequences of Ebola, SARS, bird flu, Lyme disease, and not least, AIDS. He explains the mechanics of zoonotic diseases well and cautions portentously about the Next Big One. With chilling accuracy, he predicted it would be a SARS-like coronavirus (that is airborne), rather than a retrovirus (transmitted by blood), such as the one causing AIDS. Quammen asks ominously: "When the Next Big One arrives, what will it look like? From which innocent host animal will it emerge? Will we be ready?" The last question, at least, is easy to answer: No. When the next big one came in 2020, we were not ready – but please don't say that we weren't warned.

In finance, one of my favourite analysts is James Rickards. In his book *The Death of Money: The coming collapse of the international monetary system* (2014), Rickards deals with global financial markets, geopolitics and how central bank policies and the role of the US Dollar as the world's reserve currency have led to deficit spending and debt accumulation. In his more recent *Aftermath:*

Seven secrets of wealth preservation in the coming chaos (2019), he deals in more specific terms with how investors can navigate the treacherous international financial conditions. We will look at some of the conditions that Rickards describes in a minute, such as the decades of ruinous low interest rates and debt generation, causing artificially inflated asset prices and finally inflation.

But in this context, it is interesting to note that Rickards warns about the accumulation of risks in the financial system. He points out that yes, the "100 Year Flood", to take a popular term for a low-probability calamity, is unlikely to happen next year, but over a period of 30 years the probability of it coming along is 26%. And then you must add to this a multiple of other Black Swan-type risks facing us of geopolitical, financial or "natural" nature. Such as Israel going to war with Iran, China invading Taiwan or a nuclear war between the Koreas. Then there is the possibility of a financial debt crisis, out-of-control mass migration, major power-grid collapse, cyber attacks, natural disasters – and, you guessed it, Rickards includes a worldwide pandemic among the threats. Prophetically, Rickards also lists a war between NATO and Russia among the risks to global stability; he didn't have to wait long for that one to break out either. Yes, considered on its own, Rickards said in 2019, each crisis is unlikely to happen – but taken together, considering the multiplication factor of probabilities, the next big one is "waiting right around the corner". He couldn't have been more right.

That is why, in my opinion, it is reckless when world leaders and influential decision-makers downplay systemic risk. We should do the opposite: err on the side of caution. We should face the realities, analyse the facts, and calculate the risks going forward.

Only then can we safely position ourselves, prepare mentally, take practical precautionary measures and thus be ready when the Next Big One comes along – because it will!

THE ECONOMY IS OUR FOUNDATION

With this in mind, let me stress that in my view nothing is really more important than our economy. That is why I chose to dedicate the last of my working years to advise others on how to achieve financial freedom. It worked for me, and it can work for you, if you put your mind to it and pick up the tools you need; later in the book we will see how you can do this in a sustainable fashion by joining the FIRE movement (Chapter 7).

In general I am not a great fan of Karl Marx, but I do agree with him in his assessment of what has been labelled "historical materialism", i.e. that the human means of subsistence, mode of production and macroeconomic conditions provide the foundation of any society, upon which the social structure, culture, arts and sciences are built. In the same manner, in a microeconomic sense, if you will, your own material situation as a worker and consumer provides the underpinning of your status and possibilities as a person.

While I was working in the oil business in the early 1980s, I was growing increasingly apprehensive about what we were doing. I mean, I loved my job, providing down-hole data services on drilling rigs and platforms in the Asian region, later supervising other field crews doing this. But I started wondering what the end-game of all this actually was. I saw people around me, some of my colleagues included, making good money, then spending it all without actually being better off, and with the environment where we operated paying a high price. Was it worth it? Where would it end?

In October 1985, the Prime Minister of Denmark Paul Schluter made an official visit to Singapore. As a member of the Danish diaspora, I was invited to a large event at one of the hotels one evening to meet the PM and hear him speak. In his speech, Schluter stressed that we should "get back to growth" as quickly as possible; after a decade of continuous economic growth, much of the world entered a shallow technical recession that year; Singapore's GDP fell 1.8% in 1985.[18] At the Q&A session, I asked him about something that had been on my mind for a while, that with perpetual economic growth, what was the end-game? Instead of relentless GDP growth, shouldn't we – those of us who had already reached an acceptable standard of living – slow down to protect the environment and enjoy different aspects of what constituted quality of life? The PM took my question seriously but replied that continued economic growth was necessary, mainly to lift up those who were still stuck in poverty. This has since become the standard answer from those who promote continuous and eternal economic growth, which in most countries are 99% of the influential elite.

In fairness to Schluter and others promoting economic growth, while 68.7% of the world's population lived in poverty (below $5.50/day) in 1985, by 2019, just before Covid-19 hit, that number had declined to 46.7%.[19] Hundreds of millions of people were lifted out of miserable living conditions during that period, mainly in China. But you could also argue that after almost 40 years of economic growth, the world still has some 668 million people living in extreme poverty (below $1.90/day, mainly in sub-Saharan Africa)[20]; and even more troubling, in my view, "half of the global population lives on less than US$6.85 per person per day".[21] Think about it, that is not very much to live on. How would you feel with just US$200 per month to spend?

And then there are even people out there who feel that these numbers, from the World Bank, UN and other official sources, are skewed, distorted to make the situation look better than it is. Seth Donnelly, for one, thinks so; he wrote *The Lie of Global Prosperity: How Neoliberals Distort Data to Mask Poverty and Exploitation* (2019). In the book, Donnelly acknowledges that fewer people appear to live in extreme poverty now than ever before. But he also questions the poverty metrics used by the World Bank, such as the survey techniques and the purchasing power parity conversion factors, which in his view tend to underestimate food costs for the poor. He also rebuts the assumption by World Bank economists that economic growth automatically reduces poverty – "the fairy tale about declining poverty needs to rely on increasingly sophisticated sleights-of-hand". He concludes that while the conventional Western view is that "a rising tide raises all boats", this vision "obscures the truth about growing global poverty, inequality, exploitation, and environmental destruction".

I don't think Donnelly and Schluter ever met, but they could have had an interesting discussion.

CAPITALISM ... OR WHAT?

On my part, I retired from the oil business less than a year after that brief meeting with the Danish Prime Minister. I was 33 years old. And although I have done many things since, I never worked in industry again. I spent most of the next summer, 1987, in London while my wife at the time was going through an IVF programme at a fertility clinic in Harley Street. Our twins were born early the following year.

While in London, with plenty of time on my hands, I would sometimes head down to Speaker's Corner at Hyde Park to hear some of the alternative views from people with strong opinions about our state of affairs. I even attended a rally and indoor event by some socialists; there were hundreds of people, and I thought that maybe the socialists had an answer to how our economy could be more equal and sustainable. But I must say, I didn't find the solutions there. The well-meaning British left-wingers went on and on about Karl Marx and Rosa Luxemburg and some other long-gone people I had never heard of ... What good was that going to do? I left that meeting quickly, not converted to the socialist cause and still searching for answers.

I get it, there are big problems with capitalist society. It is crisis-prone and feeds social inequality and over-consumption. The cut-throat profit motive driving expansion leaves no room for environmental consideration. If it is cheaper to dump your garbage in a lake, this is what you will do; or else your competitors will, and you are out of business. Surely there must be a better way, right? When my 2016 book came out, *Be Financially Free*, I met a few young people at events and one of them asked me if we wouldn't be better off with a government-controlled social system like in Cuba; wouldn't that be fairer and ecologically more sustainable than capitalism? I told him that I don't see people lining up at the Cuban or North Korean border to get into those countries and maybe a few other "workers' paradises" that still exist. We have to respect that every country with democratic controls also has a market-driven economic system. Like Winston Churchill said, "Democracy is the worst form of government, except for all those others that have been tried." So in a similar fashion, you could say that capitalism is the worst economic system, except for all the others.[22]

It is pretty obvious that capitalism has lifted billions of people out of despair, I accept that. Since the coal-powered steam engine was invented (mid-1700s) and later the petroleum-powered combustion engine (late 1800s), the Industrial Revolution and capitalist economic structure have improved the lives of most people. I was around to see the Berlin Wall fall in 1989; that was the period when the communist experiment in the Soviet Union after 1917 – as well as what became the Warsaw Pact countries shortly after 1945 – finally failed spectacularly and completely. I don't see East Germany or even Russia going back to how the economy used to be, prior to the fall of the Iron Curtain (1989–91). That model wasn't even that environmentally sound: the industrial pollution in the planned state-controlled economies was horrific.

Today we are stuck with capitalism, which thankfully no longer looks anything like it did just 100 years ago, prior to the Wall Street Crash of 1929 and subsequent social and market-regulatory reforms. Since then, capitalism has morphed into a mixed market economy driven by a combination of free market enter-prise with a varying element of state regulation and intervention. What we need to do is make the best of capitalism, mitigate the boom-and-bust cycles and the social inequalities inherent in the system. We need to modify the consumerism and celebration of conspicuous consumption that we no longer have the resources for. And the old colonial powers, now organized in NATO and the EU, need to snap out of their self-righteous tradition of imposing their will on others, sometimes by persuasion and pressure, at other times by sanctions and brute force.

SO, IS OUR CURRENT ECONOMY SUSTAINABLE?

With regard to sustainability, funnily enough, 1987, the year I lived in London for a while, was also the year that *Our Common Future* came out, the so-called Brundtland Report, named after the Norwegian chair of the Brundtland Commission, Dr Gro Brundtland. The commission, formed in 1983 by the UN as the World Commission for Environment and Development, was man-dated to formulate "a global agenda for change". In fact, in this report, Dr Brundtland has been credited with providing the very definition for sustainable development that has been used ever since, namely "development that meets the needs of the present without compromising the ability of future generations to meet their own needs".[23]

And yes, global change did indeed happen in the following decades. Great change for development, not so much for the environment or for sustainability. It is interesting that while the

Brundtland Report recognized that there are environmental limits to conventional economic growth in developed countries, it also had as one of its premises that poverty is not good for the environment either, as it accelerates pressure on the environment in poor regions. In my view, this contradiction is exactly what played out in the following decades. The consequence of this contradiction is that poverty is bad for the environment, and development is bad for the environment as well. We are damned if we do and damned if we don't. If we accelerate economic growth (such as China did in the decades after the report came out), the explosion in resource use ravages the country as well as surrounding regions: timber from Southeast Asia, coal from Australia, metals, sand, industrialized farming, fisheries, etc. – all destructive extractive activities. If we don't grow the economy much, as happened in parts of South Asia, sub-Saharan Africa and Latin America during the same period, the environment is denuded as well, with weak institutions allowing uncontrolled deforestation, settlements and artisanal mining; and when the natural foundation is eventually exhausted, crime, social breakdown and ultimately illegal migration to better managed areas follow.

I visited Texas and worked in the Dallas-Fort Worth area for a while in 1981. During a weekend off from work, I drove out west across the desert into nearby New Mexico. On the way to El Paso, Interstate 10 hugs the Rio Grande for some 50 miles and on the other side is Mexico. I was surprised to see how shallow this famous river was; it looked as if you could just walk across. Except no one did. There weren't many people there anyway and there was no fence and no border wall. Today, after all this economic growth and prosperity, this very same international border has become a hot-bed of illegal immigration, with hundreds of thousands of people trying to cross north into the US every month. They come from all over the Global South but mainly originate from countries in Central America ravaged by overpopulation, environmental deterioration, crime and social unrest. The recent decades of growth didn't appear to do these people much good.

The global elite have a solution for this conundrum: Green growth. The idea is that we will decouple resource extraction from economic expansion and somehow magically make everyone richer without putting more pressure on the Earth. The *relative* decoupling has indeed happened; today we use less oil and steel and such per value added to the economy. The problem is that *absolute* decoupling has not: globally, we still use more of everything. And with each notch of further GDP growth, all the numbers still go up. Relatively less, but absolutely more. Yes, in spite of digitalization, even paper consumption has gone up – by 400% over the last 40 years.[24] Emails and digital entertainment might seem less materially demanding than snail-mail letters and compact discs, but they are not without environmental impact. They just use warehouses full of computer servers and electrical power instead of paper, plastics and metal, and a lot of it. YouTube alone consumes more power-equivalent than global gold mining operations.[25]

One of the key elements in the green growth agenda is the transition to renewable energy. Hardly a day goes by where this theme is not in the news: We need to build more electric cars, powered by solar panels and wind turbines, and then we will be OK. For one, Jason Hickel does not buy this argument. Already back in 2016, he wrote an op-ed for the *Guardian* where he says: "When it comes to climate change, the problem is not just the type of energy we are using, it's what we're doing with it. What would we do with 100% clean energy? Exactly what we are doing with fossil fuels: raze more forests, build more meat farms, expand industrial agriculture, produce more cement, and fill more landfill sites, all of which will pump deadly amounts of greenhouse gas into the air."

"The root problem," Hickel points out, "is the fact that our economic system demands ever-increasing levels of extraction, production and consumption. Our politicians tell us that we need to keep the global economy growing at more than 3% each year. That means every 20 years we need to double the size of the global economy – double the cars, double the fishing, double the mining, double the McFlurries and double the iPads. And then double them again over the next 20 years from their already doubled state ... But we now have robust evidence that [GDP growth] doesn't make us happier, it doesn't reduce poverty, and its 'externalities' produce all sorts of social ills: debt, overwork, inequality, and climate change. We need to abandon GDP growth as our primary measure of progress, and we need to do this immediately."

A couple of years later, Hickel expanded on the theme of "green growth" in an op-ed in *Foreign Policy Magazine* (2018)[26]: "Ultimately, bringing our civilization back within planetary boundaries is going to require that we liberate ourselves from our dependence on economic growth – starting with rich nations. This might sound scarier than it really is. Ending growth doesn't mean shutting down economic activity – it simply means that next year we can't produce and consume more than we are doing this year. It might also mean shrinking certain sectors that are particularly damaging to our ecology and that are unnecessary for human flourishing, such as advertising, commuting, and single-use products. But ending growth doesn't mean that living standards need to take a hit. Our planet provides more than enough for all of us; the problem is that its resources are not equally distributed. We can improve people's lives right now simply by sharing what we already have more fairly, rather than plundering the Earth for more. Maybe this means better public services. Maybe it means basic income. Maybe it means a shorter working week that allows us to scale down production while still delivering full employment. Policies such as these – and countless others – will be crucial to not only surviving the 21st century but also flourishing in it."

I've jumped the gun a bit here by letting Hickel identify some of the solutions; we will get to that later. But I want to return to the theme of "green growth" and point out that Hickel is not alone when he expresses scepticism about the sustainability of this concept and our economy as a whole. If you haven't seen it already, you must watch *Planet of the Humans*, a 2019 documentary by Jeff Gibbs and supported by Michael Moore. In this show, Gibbs investigates what is behind the green energy movement, and what he finds is truly troubling: That while Tesla and Apple production facilities claim to run on 100% renewable energy, they are actually hooked up to the main grid running on coal and natural gas. Even more problematic: The solar panel and wind turbine farms are built on good old fossil fuel and mining extraction; 31 minutes into the movie, Gibbs travels to the Ivanpah Solar Array plant in the Californian Mojave Desert, which is also supported by natural gas energy, and his friend there concludes: "The whole thing is built using fossil fuel infrastructure. You use more fossil fuel than you are getting benefit from it. They would have been better off just burning the fossil fuel in the first place." When the solar panels and the wind turbines and the mirrors break down, and that happens pretty quickly, none of these materials are renewable and the whole assembly has to be rebuilt, using fossil fuels again – "if there is enough planet left", as Gibbs wryly adds. Towards the end, Gibbs concludes: "Infinite growth on a finite planet is suicide. The human presence is already beyond sustainable. It is everything we humans are doing. Less must be the new more."

Predictably, some of their fellow environmentalists, many of them deeply invested in the renewable energy industry or supported by the "green growth" lobby, came out and criticized Gibbs and Moore for their work: "Their misleading, outdated, and scientifically sophomoric dismissal of renewable energy is perhaps the most dangerous form of climate denial, eroding support for renewable energy as a critical climate solution." So said a 2020 review of the movie in *Yale Climate Connections*.[27] There are always two sides to a coin; you must make up your own mind as to which side you find more persuasive and trustworthy.

AND THEN THERE IS THE DEBT

So, in many observers' opinion, our economy build on extraction is not sustainable. Sure, we can go on finding new oil and we have iron ore to last us centuries. The problem is that the new reserves are harder to reach, so we are putting in more effort, capital and literally more energy to achieve the same results; in other words, productivity is declining. It is obvious if you think about it. When the first prospectors found gold in northern California in 1848, they literally picked big nuggets out of the edge of mountain streams using a simple pan. Some became rich beyond their wildest imagination. That attracted some 300,000 additional miners and workers and traders to the region; but as the easy gold was panned out, work became harder and harder and also more capital-intensive; the greenhorns had to dig deeper and deeper, move more and more material and found less and less; increasingly, large corporations took over, and by 1855 the area was basically mined out. Today just a few recreational prospectors work in that region, with little economic significance. You might say that productivity dropped to near zero, just like it eventually will in all industries extracting non-renewable resources such as mining, drilling and even old-growth logging.

Personally, as a finance guy, I am also concerned about our monetary conditions, specifically our addiction to debt. We simply cannot get enough of it, and it just keeps on growing. I am here referring to the world economy as a whole, not to individual small players such as Singapore, Norway and a few other prudent economies that have the political discipline to save for a rainy day.

In *Be Financially Free*, I explore the debt situation, both public and private debt expansion, so let us just look at the current situation for a quick update.

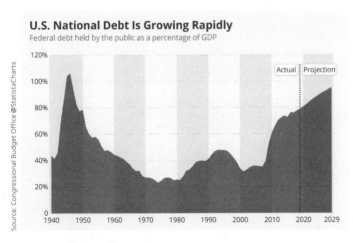

As a case in point, let us look at the debt situation in the largest and most important economy in the world, the one that issues the world's reserve currency, the US Dollar. During WWII, the US public debt was as high as it is today, in terms of percentage of GDP. The difference then was that much of the debt was actually paid back in the following years and decades, up until the oil crisis in 1973 and the Reagan years (1981–89) when the "Deficits don't matter" culture became institutionalized.

In nominal terms, the growth in American public debt is even more astonishing. I graduated from high school in 1971; look at the debt level then, compared to now!

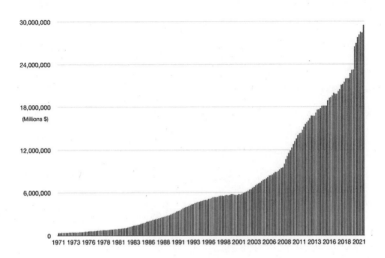

And then there is private consumer debt. We didn't have much of that when I was born in 1952, but look at us now. I know this is the US, but the trend would be the same for virtually any country you might select, I can assure you – yes, even China.

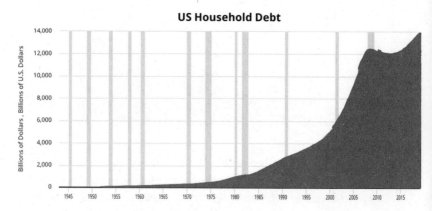

US Household Debt

So my question is: If we are so rich now, if we have grown so much since the 1950s and we have all this stuff to show for it, how come we still owe money? Shouldn't you pay your debt back as you make more money? You shouldn't take on more debt, should you? Then you are not really richer at all, you are just deeper in debt – am I right or am I right?

If you watch most of the talking heads on financial television, which I often do late at night when markets are open in the West and I am too tired to do anything else, you won't hear much about the debt crisis. Here, the mantra is: We just need to get back to growth. "Debt ceiling" is a dirty word in those circles – a ceiling must be avoided at all costs – and paying the debt down is labelled "austerity" and frowned upon. The effect is that we are wrecking the Earth not just on borrowed time but also on borrowed capital.

When I say "most", I don't mean all. Occasionally a sensible person is allowed to appear in public – he or she would usually then be labelled a contrarian. American economist Nouriel Roubini is one of those, enough of an insider to be allowed airtime, but also enough of a financial maverick to tell it as he sees it. Dr Roubini wrote *Megathreats* (2022), where he lists 10 serious threats to global financial stability – the first chapter is called "The Mother of All Debt Crises". The other issues he deals with are monetary policies, demographics, stagflation, currency meltdowns, the AI threat, the new Cold War … and yes, the last threat-chapter is called "An Uninhabitable Planet?". Towards the end of the book, as he addresses the question of whether this disaster can be averted, Roubini tries to be positive as most authors usually do (optimism always sells better than realism), and his last chapter is titled "A More 'Utopian' Future?". However, somehow you can feel his heart is not really in this rose-coloured message, as the previous chapter, "Dark Destiny", is so much more convincingly written. Basically, Dr Roubini does not think the debt crisis will end well.

Another one of my favourite financial analysts, Peter Schiff, doesn't buy into the debt euphoria either. He believes that something will have to give. He doesn't quite know what or when, but he urges his supporters to stay vigilant. Some years back, he predicted that the policy pursued by the US Federal Reserve of ultra-low interest rates would eventually result in inflation and/or a devaluation of the USD. Well, during and after the Covid-19 pandemic, inflation did indeed start to manifest itself, and beginning in March 2022, the Fed did start hiking the Federal Funds Rate to fight inflation; central banks in the EU and other major economies have started to follow suit.

Specifically to Singapore, as you might know, the central bank, the Monetary Authority of Singapore (MAS), does not set interest rates, like central banks do in most other developed economies. Given Singapore's open, trade-dependent financial system, MAS conducts monetary policy primarily by tweaking the rate of the currency, the SGD, compared to a basket of currencies from Singapore's main trading partners, with the USD supposedly carrying a high weight in this equation. Hence MAS tightens (i.e. increases) the value of the SGD to put a brake on the economy during times of high inflation, and pauses or lowers its value during a slowdown or recessionary crisis to stimulate local demand and investment. Interest rates charged for bank loans and mortgages are set by the local banks themselves, in effect following international rates.

The generally higher interest rates have caused some business failures from technology start-ups depending on cheap capital and some banks that are now insolvent, as higher interest rates mean lower prices on those bonds that the banks typically hold as reserves. When Silicon Valley Bank failed a year after the Fed started raising rates, this was a warning to financial markets that there was instability in the system.

If you listen to Peter Schiff and other contrarians, this is only the beginning of a new major financial crisis and/or a period of stagflation (meaning an inflationary environment as well as zero to negative growth in the aggregate economy). And/or it is the beginning of the end to the US Dollar's role as the world's reserve currency. However, if you believe the mainstream talking suits and government officials, in case of a recession, the central banks around the world can just lower the interest rates back down to near zero – without rekindling inflation presumably! – then issue some more debt, and all will be well. The rest of us? We will just have to see how this all pans out. Later I will give you some ideas about how to protect your assets in both scenarios.

CAN WE REACH A STEADY STATE?

Earlier in this chapter, I referred at some length to the work of Jason Hickel. In 2020, he published *Less is More: How Degrowth Will Save the World*.

Degrowth. This is a concept explored by some economists concerned about the fact that continued expansion in a confined space is not mathematically or practically possible. Professor Herman Daly is regarded as the pioneer of this kind of analysis. While acknowledging that continuous growth is not possible, the same could be said for continuous degrowth, so in the 1970s Daly developed a concept he called the "steady-state economy" and was active in the field of Ecological Economics.

There are basically two schools providing an alternative to conventional economics dealing with macroeconomic concepts such as monetary and fiscal policies and trade issues, as well as microeconomics covering business matters like demand and supply functions and price discovery:

1. Environmental Economics is considered the "weaker" of the two; this school accepts that the environment matters, but finds tools within conventional economic theory to deal with them, such as tweaking

pricing in the system with penalties and subsidies to achieve a better environmental outcome.

2. Ecological Economics is the "stronger" of the two sub-fields; it rejects the concept of continuous expansion and prioritizes the preservation of natural capital to protect overall quality of life.

This was Daly's field, Ecological Economics, and he won much recognition and many awards for his work. In my view, conventional economics academia has let us down: not enough emphasis has been put on finding solutions to our existential environmental issues by economic and financial experts. There is so much brain-power there, at the universities and business schools, so many sophisticated theoretical tools and models available, and yet they mainly prioritize one thing, and one thing only: How can we squeeze yet more value out of a completely exhausted natural system that is the foundation for everything else. In *Enough is Enough: Building a Sustainable Economy in a World of Finite Resources* (2013), Rob Dietz and Dan O'Neil agree with me; after 10 years, their book still seems to me the most accessible and relevant guide to the subject of economic sustainability.

So there are some qualified people out there looking at alternative models for development, incorporating sustainable accountability and considering the planet's limitations. In 2022, several of them joined hands and collectively wrote an article in *Nature*[28]: "Degrowth can work ... Wealthy economies should abandon growth of gross domestic product (GDP) as a goal, scale down destructive and unnecessary forms of production to reduce energy and material use, and focus economic activity around securing human needs and well-being. This approach, which has gained traction in recent years, can enable rapid decarbonization and stop ecological breakdown while improving social outcomes. It frees up energy and materials for low- and middle-income countries in which growth might still be needed for development. Degrowth is a purposeful strategy to stabilize economies and achieve social and ecological goals, unlike recession, which is chaotic and socially destabilizing and occurs when growth-dependent economies fail to grow."

But anyway, I live in Singapore and in the local context we don't have to worry too much about all this. Here, the economy – as measured by annual change in GDP – will continue to grow; multiple generations of political leaders are committed to this: "Even as Singapore is shifting towards a new phase that emphasizes a more inclusive concept of success and caring for all members of society, economic growth will continue to be a 'non-negotiable', Deputy Prime Minister Lawrence Wong said. As the labour force and economy are both expected to grow more slowly in the years ahead, competitiveness will become more, not less, important, he added. If Singapore does not grow the economic pie, there will be fewer jobs and less scope for social support, he said."[29]

I am in no position to argue with this. It would never cross my mind to contradict a politician. My mother served more than 20 years in the Danish Parliament, so I know that politicians have a hard job. Every four or five years, they must face the electorate in a gruelling general election. I don't envy politicians one bit and I would not like to be in their shoes. I cannot even vote at elections; that is because I am not a resident where I am a citizen, and I am not a citizen where I am a resident! So for the rest of us, those of us outside of party politics, I hope we can still have an opinion and express it, but we cannot demand or dictate what should be done. Luckily there are many other ways to have influence: as a worker, as an investor, as a consumer, as a volunteer – we will look at some of that next.

3

Work and Productivity

In the last chapter, we saw how the pursuit of economic growth is inevitable going forward. I quoted a few academics based in Western countries like the US, UK and Canada working on alternative development models incorporating temporary degrowth in rich territories, until global steady-state equilibrium can be reached. But this school of thought has never gained traction in mainstream economic theory, nor in politics. Singapore's DPM Lawrence Wong is not alone in categorically rejecting any notion of a stop to growth: economic growth is non-negotiable.

I get the point. In fact, there is some truth to it; who am I or Jason Hickel to tell the poor people that we have to stop growing the economic pie? If you look at the world as a whole, half the people, as we saw earlier, live on less than $6.85 per day. Will someone with just $200 to spend each month support a steady-state economy? It would be arrogant to presume. Even in the rich countries, voters do not accept degrowth. Take France, for instance: this important old colonial power's fiscal position is untenable. But when the government in 2023 proposed to raise the state pension age from 62 to 64 to reduce the budget deficit, did voters welcome the idea? Did they say, "Right, finally a sensible move to ensure sustainability, reduce consumption and protect the future environment"? No, of course not; they rallied in the streets by the millions, demanding more free money and fighting with the police, just like the French do whenever the government suggests a reduction in farming subsidies or higher taxes on diesel. In a democracy, an elected government promoting financial discipline and environmental sustainability will not stay elected for very long.

In a way it is kind of paradoxical. We look at the GDP numbers and they are always up and up and up. Among development economists and anthropologists, 1950 is considered the start of what has been labelled the Great Acceleration, when global GDP growth took off, initially in the West but later worldwide, including the Global South.

But my point is, if we are 10 times richer now than when I was born, why do we have to work more? Why do the French raise the pension age? Why are we told that we have to retire later? If we are doing so well now finally, shouldn't we kick back and work less and enjoy life? Or am I missing something?

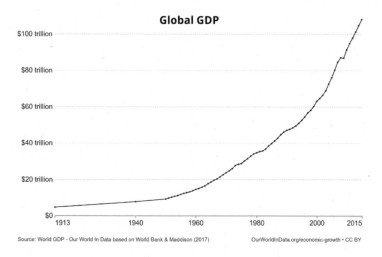

Source: World GDP - Our World In Data based on World Bank & Maddison (2017)   OurWorldInData.org/economic-growth • CC BY

I was born in 1952, at the start of the Great Acceleration, when everything shot up. This graph is global GDP, adjusted for inflation and expressed in 2011 USD prices. But a graph showing production, consumption, investment, urbanization, trade, telecommunication, transportation and international travel would have the same shape. In 70 years, global real GDP has gone up tenfold, from under $10 trillion to over $100 trillion.

The new reality is that these numbers do not show that much of what constitutes economic growth today is in fact not economic; it is *uneconomic growth*, i.e. economic activity that inflates the GDP numbers without generating much additional utility or quality of life. It is growth that "produces negative externalities which reduce the overall quality of life. The negative social and environmental consequences outweigh the short-term value of an extra unit of growth, making it uneconomic."[30] I will get back to the consequences of some of that a little later.

THE EVOLVING JOB MARKET

In such an economic environment, our new reality means that what we do to generate value and earn a living has changed as well, and this change will only continue going forward. Other volumes in this book series will deal in more detail with what constitutes the future of work. But from my point of view, it is important to emphasize that "work" has never been a static, well-defined entity. When I grew up in Copenhagen, Denmark, we had a telephone operator connect our calls. You would call the telephone exchange, talk to a person and ask for the number you wanted to be connected to. At the other end of the line, I suppose a bunch of ladies would pull the telephone jack out and connect it to another socket, like you see them do in old movies. This was in a million-people city – the man-hours (or woman-hours) going into this must have been substantial. In the following years, this system was gradually automated and all the telephone operators were out of a job.

At that time, big companies and government agencies had a large pool of workers – the typing pool – to type out correspondence on manual, later electrical, typewriters and mail out letters. The typing pool was also mainly ladies, so what did the men do? Well, many worked on farms; in 1952, 24% of the Danish labour force was employed in agriculture[31]; today the number is just 2–3%, and this transformation would have been the same in most developed countries. Since there was less international trade and most products were made domestically, there were jobs in small manufacturing, large factories and labour-intensive heavy industries such as shipbuilding. The shipyards and shoe factories have long gone from Denmark and much of Europe.

When I was a kid, in the 1960s and even into the 70s, we always had the option of dropping out of school and going to work, cleaning bottles at the local Carlsberg brewery, or take a stint on a Maersk merchant vessel. That kind of work didn't pay much, but it was always available. Not so today: what few factories are left in Denmark are mainly automated and the sailor jobs have been taken over by Filipinos and Bangladeshis.

But that doesn't mean that there isn't work to be done or money to be made. It just means that the job market is constantly evolving and that workers have to understand all the moving parts involved and then position themselves accordingly. In Denmark, and in much of Western Europe, and the US as well, most of the jobs I mention above are gone forever. But the amount of work in an economy is not a fixed number; new jobs will emerge, new assignments will need to be filled. I am somewhat pessimistic about many aspects of our economy structure, but not about the labour market. Maybe that is because I have seen it transformed radically in a very short time. Some jobs disappear, but other jobs take their place. If you are flexible and keep an ear to the ground, you will be able to identify new trends and new opportunities.

I still have friends in the oil and gas service industry and we meet up once in a while. Most of them have retired now, like I did long ago. One commented that toward the end of his career he got a bit tired of having to reinvent himself every few years. When desktop computers came out in the late 1970s, in our company we were some of the first field hands to bring computer power to the rigs; otherwise the instrumentation at the time was all analog. We would set up a Hewlett-Packard data processing system in our portable cabin on the deck and connect a signal cable via the rig floor to the electronic gauges we lowered into the bottom of the well. We taught ourselves some basic computer language skills to modify the monitoring programmes ourselves. Over the decades that followed, my friend had to reinvent himself numerous times, learning new tools, new techniques and new computer languages. In his early 60s he finally had enough of that and retired on his (by that time, substantial) savings. He told me he would advise young people today to get a classical education in arts or languages; those skills never get old! If you can play Mozart or Beethoven or teach ancient Roman history, you can build up your knowledge continuously like a multi-storey mansion, instead of having to tear all your knowledge apart and discard it like a prefabricated bungalow, then rebuild the structure from scratch every few years.

In all fairness, another one of my former colleagues loves technology to this day; he found the constant changes and upgrades stimulating. "Technology is my friend, this is how I made my living," he says, and although he is retired now, he is one of those who spends his time studying the complicated features of new IT and communication gadgets and queues up when the latest Samsung smartphone is available. Another friend even still works for the American oil-service giant Halliburton, although I am sure he doesn't need the money, with the kids long gone and the house paid for years ago. A pleasant working environment is essential for him: "The day they give me a boss I can't stand, I will quit," he says. Obviously that hasn't happened yet.

SO, WHAT IS "WORK"?

People can easily grasp that quitting your job is a major decision, a life-changing event. But so is staying in the same job; that is a decision you make as well, even if it doesn't seem so obvious. Your time, your working life, is limited and there is an opportunity cost to staying where you are. In other words, the time you spend at that job could alternatively have been spent doing another job, or nothing at all! I have a son born in 2002, a Gen Z. At the moment he is about to decide what he wants to do with his future; it is an exciting period in any young person's life. Should I go with a technical education and join the IT frenzy, stay with the classical learning that never goes out of style or latch on to the "sustainability" craze and learn environmental engineering?

In our family, we have an interesting mix of age groups. We are all navigating various stages of working life. Since I am in effect retired now, I can only reflect back and conclude that work is a funny thing, and the secret to a fulfilling working life is to find your passion and make it pay. As the saying goes: "If you do what you love, you'll never work a day in your life."

I have heard that some people pay money to go on a safari in East Africa to drive around with a guide and photograph the wildlife. Personally, I find that hard to believe. That sort of thing is work, isn't it? In 2002 and 2003, a company, Private Wilderness, flew me on business class from Singapore to Kenya, then by private plane into the bush; there they put me up at a number of luxurious savannah resorts. At each place I was given a Land Rover and a private driver and wildlife guide and then I set about photographing the birds of that area. Back in Singapore, I would edit the photographs, write the captions and produce an illustrated bird guide and checklist for each destination. Private Wilderness paid me well, so I suppose that was work, even though I enjoyed every minute of it.

Likewise, there are people in the world who get paid handsomely to play tennis or golf or videogames, while others have to pay to do the same thing. Virtually every hobby you can think of could also be a job, such as gardening, fishing or playing a musical instrument. So turn your passion into your profession. But any job will have its downside too, even your dream job, such as dealing with the occasional difficult customer, chasing a stingy client for payments long overdue, or sending out stuff that got lost in the mail. In every job or assignment, you should be mentally prepared to deal with setbacks, even if in general you're doing what you love.

IS AI GOOD OR BAD?

We saw how some jobs got lost during economic and social change, while others were created to take their place. Remember the 24% of the workforce employed in the agricultural sector in Denmark 70 years ago? Well, today, there are far fewer farms in Denmark (33,000 versus 400,000 in 1950), and the area under farming has shrunk by 15%. And yet, paradoxically, today a lot more food is produced by the 2–3% of the workforce left in the sector; it has been said that Denmark could feed 20 million people (they are only 5.6 million themselves). What has happened is an exponential increase in productivity, measured both as output per person as well as output per land area under cultivation.[32]

And Denmark is not unique in this regard. This graph plotting output versus employment from the UK shows the astonishing productivity gain in the farming sector.

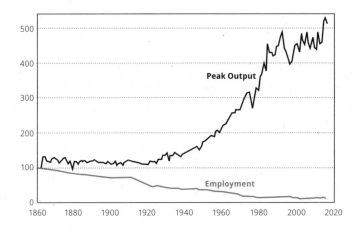

A graph illustrating the trend in the UK manufacturing sector would show a similar picture: output up while employment down, although the discrepancy is not as astonishing as on the farms.

Not only that, but to get back to the case of Denmark, out of the people leaving the farming sector, and their descendants, many went into totally different new occupations, such as IT services, and today the export of computer software products exceeds the value of Denmark's farm exports, important as this business still is for the country. Out of total exports, intangible "services" now constitute almost half (46%) of all exports, while real stuff, goods, are the other half (53%).[33] I am sure a similar development could be identified for most countries in the world.

Judging from all this, while old-school jobs may disappear, they are being replaced with brand new ones. I am not in the

"Technology will eat our lunch" camp, but many others are. As Nouriel Roubini, one of my favourite financial analysts, says in his book *Megathreats* (2022): "Algorithms that learn on their own can do many more jobs once thought exempt from mechanization. Anyone who monitors data, whether doctors, lawyers, teachers, or forest rangers, must compete with mind-boggling computing power that scans and remembers vast amounts of data, and then might propose unconventional responses. AI encroaches on more jobs than in prior revolutions. All this is why the AI revolution may be the first one that destroys overall jobs and wages. Complacency this time – the assumption that once again, the Luddites will be wrong – looks like a fatal mistake."

The "Luddite" reference is to a group of textile workers in early Industrial Revolution England who around 1779 started smashing new textile weaving machinery. The new automated industrial machinery left many workers unemployed, as fewer workers were needed to produce new and better and cheaper goods. Sounds familiar? Ever since, the Luddites have come to represent workers resisting technological progress and automation.

So, the Luddites were wrong. Over the long run, automation and technological innovation vastly improved overall industrial output, product quality, productivity and eventually – even though it took a long time – worker welfare. But now we are being told that "This time it is different", again. Will it really be different?

It seems that the jury is still out on this. And while the jury members are considering the case, the prosecutor's office is represented by people like Dr Roubini and Peter Schiff. Schiff is sceptical of the benefits of AI; he says it will not fix our problems, such as those with the environment; we will still need steel and cars and stuff. Others, like Bill Gates, are on the defence team. "I've been thinking a lot about how AI can reduce some of the world's worst inequities," he writes.[34] In the field of healthcare, for example, AI will "dramatically accelerate the rate of medical breakthroughs." In agriculture, "AIs can help develop better seeds based on local conditions, advise farmers on the best seeds to plant based on the soil and weather in their area, and help develop drugs and vaccines for livestock." In education, AI-driven software will "know your interests and your learning style so it can tailor content that will keep you engaged. It will measure your understanding, notice when you're losing interest, and understand what kind of motivation you respond to". Gates concludes: "We're only at the beginning of what AI can accomplish. Whatever limitations it has today will be gone before we know it." Finally: "Put in your order for new overpriced AI products from Microsoft tomorrow." No, sorry, I added that last part!

Daniel Susskind is not really prosecuting or defending; you could consider him an expert witness in the "AI versus the People" case. Dr Susskind is a British academic who wrote *A World Without Work: Technology, Automation and How We Should Respond* (2021), and he sums up our situation by saying that the new technologies are indeed replacing some jobs, but also creating many new ones. Only this time it really is a bit different: "Technology is creating lots of jobs for people to do. But for various reasons, people aren't able to move into those jobs." And this is not a problem for the future; we have to accept that this is happening right now. "We are already facing a serious skills mismatch, because we are creating jobs that people don't necessarily have the skills to do."[35]

Finally, there is big business. What do they think of AI? Business doesn't get much bigger than Goldman Sachs; they put out a report in March 2023 where they concluded that AI would replace the equivalent of 300 million full-time jobs, but also declared AI a "major advancement" that would add 7% to global GDP.[36] As reported by the BBC, the statement said that some sectors were more vulnerable than others: 46% of tasks in administrative and 44% in legal professions could be automated, but only 6% in construction, 4% in maintenance. The report found that 60% of workers are in occupations that did not exist in 1940, so disruption is nothing new. Only lately, since 1980, research suggests that in some sectors, technological change has displaced workers faster than it has created jobs. And it has forced down wages in others: "Consider the introduction of GPS technology and platforms like Uber. Suddenly, knowing all the streets in London had much less value – and so incumbent drivers experienced large wage cuts in response, of around 10% according to our research. The result was lower wages, not fewer drivers."

THE TECHNO CHANGE: BRING IT ON!

My take on the technological revolution and AI is: Bring it on. Maybe it's because I lived through the transformation from analog to digital technology and it was amazing. When I served in a 155mm artillery battery in the army during my national service, I was put in charge of calculating the coordinates of our firing position. Other teams operated the howitzers themselves and directed the fire. Me and my guys found the coordinates, rain or shine, day or night, in 20 minutes or less using maps, measuring tape, an electric gyroscope and ... wait for it: logarithmic tables to calculate the trigonometric variables! 20 minutes? And we thought we were pretty good with that. Today this operation would take 20 seconds with a handheld GPS gadget.

I wrote my first books on a mechanical typewriter, using liquid paper to make corrections; the word processor really only got into common use during the early 1980s. When I went to school, we didn't even have pocket calculators. We used multiplication tables and a slide rule to calculate stuff. I bought my first Sony walkman when I arrived in Singapore in 1980; before that we only had the transistor radio; you certainly couldn't pick your own music on the go. If you wanted to see a movie, you went to the movie theatre. I got my first video cassette player for home movies only in the early 1980s as well.

So has technology improved the lives of us Baby Boomers? You bet it has. It has given us so many more choices, improved the speed and efficiency of both work and leisure. But I must say, I have maintained an ounce of skepticism during all this. On the rigs, while I was working in petroleum engineering, we did a calculation called a Horner plot during the DST, drill stem testing, of a new well. As I mentioned, my company was one of the first to bring computers to location and do the on-site analysis. The client loved it when we had the plotter working during the test, plotting each data point in real time to approximate the p* value, the static reservoir pressure. There was only one problem with that: I always felt that my manual calculation using a sharp pencil on a sheet of graph paper was more accurate. While the computer just extrapolated the data automatically, I could read from the speed and regularity, and occasionally irregularity, of data what p* was most likely to be, judging by experience from all the other tests I had seen. The client always preferred the computer's results, although I was convinced my manual method was better.

What I mean is, people can do some things better than machines. That is why, in my view, we will always need people. Will improved algorithms, AI and further automation continue? No doubt. That means that going forward, more tasks in healthcare, education and transportation can be done by computers. But I can assure you, we will always need doctors – real people to talk to and to examine and treat us. We will always need real teachers to inspire and mentor young people. And if some buses should one day be made autonomous, that is fine with me; on my part, I will always prefer to drive my own car. My wife and I did a road trip through Sweden and Norway in the summer of 2022. At Arlanda Airport, Stockholm, the car rental company gave me this Hyundai plug-in hybrid to drive. I never used the plug-in functions – I found all the cables and the procedures cumbersome; I just filled some gas in the tank now and then as I always have done. It would have been more environmentally friendly to do away with all the elec-tric motor stuff and big batteries and cables and just use a small combustion engine to power the car; I will get back to that later in Chapter 6. But regarding AI, the brand-new vehicle had an auto-steering function that was supposed to keep the car in its lane on the highway. I found that feature incredibly annoying – dangerous, in fact! It was as if someone was sitting next to me, randomly jerking the steering wheel this way and that. After every start-up, I had to manually disengage this function. I was the des-ignated driver on that trip; we covered 2,515 km in all. My wife helped out with navigation, and I must say that the GPS screen in the vehicle as well as her smartphone navigation app were pretty amazing. We only took a wrong turn once, and that was because I used my own intuition and ignored instructions. I shouldn't have, because the lady on the phone turned out to be right! So some innovations make our lives better, others are just a nuisance.

Sometimes it helps to be old; you view developments with a longer perspective, your horizon is a bit further out, and thus you are less likely to get caught up in the fashionable flavour of the moment. I have lost count of all the inventions that did *not* work out, in my lifetime alone. Remember the *Back to the Future II* movie from 1989, the scene from 2015? That Hoverboard, it never really happened, did it? At least, I have never seen one – or any of the other stuff we would supposedly have by now. I grew up in the 1960s with the American series *The Jetsons*. In this futuristic cartoon, Mr Jetson works one hour per day, two days per week, his wife doesn't work, and yet they have a comfortable life with robots doing all the chores and their own flying car. Sixty years later, we are still talking about those flying cars – we will get them one day, soon – and I have still never seen a real robot in action anywhere. So I take the doomsday prospects of AI and robots taking over the world with a grain of salt.

Oh, yes. I saw what you might call a robot cleaning the floor the other day at the MRT (Mass Rapid Transit) station. There was a guy controlling the robot from a distance; he might as well have cleaned the floor himself. The coffee shop down the road for a while tried out an automatic door opening system. It broke down and now we push the door open again. The change-dispensing machine they had for a while also didn't work, so now we get the change manually as we always did. At our estate, the out-door lights are supposed to come on from 7 pm to 7 am, but this mechanism has never worked consistently as long as we have stayed here. Half the time the lights are on for much of the day, completely wasting the fossil fuel energy that drives them. The "smart city" people still have a lot of work to do.

And now we are supposed to worry about AI? Excuse me if I don't buy into this. So, ChatGPT can write some boring essay based on general information available? Be my guest. AI could never write my book. Let the machines do all the trifling stuff if they want to, we people can take care of the fun part. Albert Einstein has been quoted as saying, "Never memorize something that you can look up."[37] I couldn't agree more. Of course, for the "looking up" bit, Einstein was referring to libraries and dictionaries, but today, with everyone carrying all the world's knowledge on their smartphones everywhere they go, that statement is more relevant than ever. So the computers can store all the trivial information; it is much easier that way. We people will handle the creative and inspiring parts of life.

ARE WE RUNNING ON THE SPOT?

More important to me than who does what – machines or people – is the overall picture and the sustainability of it all. In the next couple of chapters, we will look at this in more detail, but it appears to me that much of the technological progress that we have enjoyed the benefits of during the Great Acceleration (since 1950) has been built on a shaky foundation. The process has been very capital-intensive, and for the last few decades more and more of this capital is generated out of thin air, by expanding the money supply and creating more debt, as we saw in the previous chapter. Much of the technological "innovation" has been a desperate attempt by technology start-ups to find a market for products we really don't need. This was OK for many years, especially so after the 2007–2008 Financial Crisis and subsequent expansion of monetary and fiscal stimulus. But when inflation finally caught up with the 0% (or in Europe, even negative) interest rate regimes in 2022, the start-ups made possible mainly by a free flow of cash started suffering, many going belly-up.

I mean, I like to exercise, I walk up all the staircases I come across (and in Singapore we have a lot of those!); I also hike, bicycle, do chin-ups and swim. None of these activities cost me anything. I don't need anything from Peloton Interactive, Inc., thank you. Peloton is an American firm that makes super-expensive exercise equipment, complete with access to the internet, livestreaming functions and built-in sensors to monitor your performance. Sorry, I prefer a nice walk in the woods looking at the critters to this hysterical data overload. Peloton had their heyday after 0% interest rates were introduced and especially during the Covid-19 pandemic, which favoured home-based activities, often of a technological nature.

Maybe Jason Hickel is right when he says that there are large sections of the economy we don't really need. I just prefer it when this adjustment is done by market demand, or the lack of it. Let the consumer decide, as long as the economy is a level playing field where you can make well-informed choices. We don't really need a Big Brother government to tell us what we need or don't need. After 2021, consumers and investors changed their mind on Peloton, and the lofty share valuations dropped to more realistic levels.

The end of free money in 2022 saw a shake-up of the whole technology space; in the next couple of chapters we will see what the implications for investors are, but here let us just stay with the productivity and sustainability angle for a bit longer.

When I first came to Singapore in 1980, there was a large gap between wages and living standards in the West and some of the countries where I was sent to do field work, such as Indonesia and Thailand. Today there are still global social inequalities, the way Seth Donnelly, Jason Hickel and others describe them, but for the middle class in Europe and much of Asia, the gap has closed. At that time, a local colleague of mine, while we were doing a survey in Indonesia, asked me about something that had puzzled him: Why did a bus driver in Indonesia make so much less than a bus driver in Europe? I could see his point. They do exactly the same job, yet a bus driver in Denmark at the time could live in his own little house, drive a car, support a family and have a pretty decent life. There was no way an Indonesian driver could live like that; he had to get by on a few dollars per day. The secret to that is supply and demand of labour and productivity. Productivity, i.e. output per hour worked, over time generates value and builds up wealth in the society; the formation of capital then enables investments, further expansion and finally higher welfare and quality of life.

Here is a case story about productivity from real life. When I lived in Denmark for a few years in the 1990s, I was driving home to the suburbs one day and pulled into a Statoil gas station outside of town to fill up the car. It was on a sprawling piece of land with three rows of pumps, a large minimart, and an auto car wash round the back. That day I topped up the tank and walked into the station to pay and saw to my surprise that the neighbour's teenage daughter was at the counter; she was the only one in the whole place. I knew she was in high school, so I gathered that this was her part-time after-school gig. I asked if it was really safe for a young girl like her to woman this place all on her own, but she said: "I have no problem with that. It is only that they will probably fire me soon. I turn 18 in a few months and by law the company will have pay me more, full adult minimum wage, so they will find another younger teenager to replace me." Today, down the road from my place in Singapore, we have a Caltex station on a small piece of land surrounded by other buildings – land is at a premium here. But people are not. At the counter, taking payment and selling cigarettes and snacks, are two women, sometimes three. There is a manager in the back office. Two elderly geezers wait outside at the pumps to fill up for you. The car wash has two to three guys washing cars; another lady dries the vehicles by hand when they come out. There are eight grown-ups to do what one teenager in Denmark did. Of course that one person has a higher productivity; it is all about supply of labour and automation.

As we saw historically with agriculture, but also with manufacturing and services, technology and capital input have played a big part in that expansion leading to higher productivity. However, lately, in this century, there are signs that this productivity increase has slowed down, and in many sectors come to a halt. Much of our current activity generates little of real value and is uneconomic and pointless. Jeff Bezos, founder and executive chairman of Amazon, made real money selling books and diapers and server space and everything else under the sun to consumers; then in July 2021 he spent $5.5 billion (billion, with a "b") of that on a 4-minute joyride, in a rocket sending him and a few friends out to the edge of the atmosphere and back.[38] Richard Branson did the same trick the same month. Maybe Branson would have been better off saving the money from that trip for a rainy day; in April 2023 his space company, Virgin Orbit Holdings Inc., went belly-up.

Personally I think that space exploration is exciting and important. The use of satellite technology has revolutionized many aspects of our lives. I just don't really think that people need to go up there; let the robots do the work! The dream of Elon Musk to colonize Mars is not only unrealistic but quite frankly erroneous and downright irresponsible. It is especially wrong when taxpayer funds, via the American federal space agency NASA, are channelled into wasteful projects. I am sure I was not the only one in the world who found it distasteful when control room staff cheered wildly as the SpaceX Starship, built to bring people out to settle in space, failed 4 minutes into its first test flight in April 2023; the 120m-long, 5-ton rocket disintegrated and burnt up after take-off, but the launch was nevertheless deemed a success! We will just build some more of those and try again, the message from Elon Musk was. My message is: No, please don't. We don't have the resources for this. It is not sustainable.

Sending a man to the Moon again, in 2025 or 2026 – that seems to be the plan. How original is that? I didn't even bother to watch the first time around. That was in July 1969 and I was in Lapland, Sweden, photographing birds that month. As a young man, I found the whole event fairly pointless and inconsequential. My high school friends and I were worried about other things, such as the Vietnam War, environmental deterioration, racism and colonialism, getting hold of the latest albums by Jimi Hendrix and the Doors. With the moon landing, nothing of importance to us was really accomplished. So is that the best humanity can come up with now, a repeat of this meaningless government-funded endeavour?

If we really aim for sustainability, we need to think carefully about how we allocate limited financial capital, as well as natural resources, going forward. Like the rest of the economy, technology needs to reach a steady state where we can meet the needs of the present without compromising the ability of future generations to meet their own needs, to quote Gro Brundtland's definition of sustainability again. That transformation should be voluntary and democratic, driven by informed choices made by voters and workers and consumers; governments can help and facilitate reform, but should not force the process.

The "green jobs" will be there – it is important that we get young people engaged in sustainability efforts and conservation and habitat restoration projects. There is work to be done. From a strictly economic point of view, maybe the output per input will not be quite what we were used to in the "bad old days" during the extractive economy. It is a sad fact that most likely you make more money from cutting a primary rainforest and selling the wood to the Americans or the Chinese than you do from letting it stay and then guide a few tourists in once in a while to look at the monkeys. Although more sustainable, that latter activity most likely will have lower productivity. So that is why it is especially important, going forward, that you manage your personal savings well, to preserve and grow your capital and to live a life doing what you love. We will look at how you can set up a sustainable investment portfolio next.

4

The Sustainable Investment Portfolio

WHAT TO DO WITH ALL THE MONEY

So, let us assume that you navigated the new economy and job market and ended up making some money. What do you do with it? First of all: Don't spend it all, please! I know that it can be hard to control your spending when you first start making a buck. There is pressure from peers and advertisers bombarding you with suggestions of stuff to buy and places to go; internet shopping firms like Amazon make it so easy to click and order and pay for gadgets and knick-knacks you don't need. So before you hit the "Buy" button, ask yourself, not "Do I want this?", but "Can I live without this?". And if the answer is yes, close the screen. Not only do you do yourself a favour, but you also help the environment, by reducing the aggregate demand for energy and non-renewable resources.

Keep your money for a rainy day. Because it *will* rain; unlike Janet Yellen, I am here to tell you, you *will* see another crisis in your lifetime – financial, environmental, social, or all of the above. I can assure you of that, because we are already in one. Besides, applying the principle of delayed gratification can be tremendously rewarding in itself. It is an acquired skill. Small children don't know how to do this, but grownups should learn. If you stash your money away, it will always be there, provided you know how to manage it. Seeing it grow, seeing your financial muscle build up, can be marvellously rewarding. With a bit of luck – and some skill – you will have so much more to spend when the time comes to buy a car or a house or help your children one day.

But how do you keep your money, how do you invest it? This question is on a lot of people's minds, young and old. When people hear that I have financial advisory qualifications, it usually doesn't take long before the question comes up: How do you think I should invest?

Most people don't really expect to get rich overnight, or even quick. Some do, but those I cannot really help – they will have to go somewhere else for an opinion. My experience is that what investors generally want is an alternative to keeping cash in the bank. Let me right away clarify that in finance, "cash" is used to describe not only physical bank notes and coins, but all liquid funds that can be accessed on short notice, such as bank checking accounts; the term "cash and cash equivalents" includes short-term securities that can be sold from one day to the next, such as money market funds and government bonds with a duration of less than 90 days.

As you move out from there, further up the investment curve, your assets become less liquid, more difficult to access in a hurry. But you really have to do that ... invest. I tell friends that I cannot predict how the markets will move tomorrow, or next month, or next year. Nobody knows that for certain, although the financial industry is filled to the brim with "experts" who pretend they do. But I can promise you one thing with certainty: If you keep your money in the bank, or under the mattress, it will inevitably become worth less and less over time. At the moment, and for many years now, this has even been the same thing, with the banks offering 0% interest on a current account. For a while in Europe (2014–21), the bank rates were even negative, in a bizarre historical anomaly that I will not get into here; in that case the cash-under-the-mattress storage method was actually a better choice. But the bottom line is, in a capitalist economy, the amount of capital will always go up, as will prices; commercial banks will never give you a real return on a current account ("real" meaning nominal rate minus inflation); they have to make money themselves. To put it simply: Inflation will eat up your cash, slowly but surely. So to protect yourself in the long run, you have to learn how to invest.

A SUPER-QUICK FINANCE PRIMER

First, to get a higher return on your capital, you can consider putting your money in a fixed deposit; a bank or licensed finance company can arrange this for you. This is – like cash – considered a risk-free investment and preferred by risk-averse individuals, as well as organizations such as societies and condominium management councils, which are often under regulatory rules to avoid financial risk. All you have to do is shop around for the best rate and decide for how long you want to tie up your capital, typically six months or a year. By then you can roll over your deposit at the prevailing interest rate or cash out. Study the terms; usually your money will be liquid and you can get out of and cancel the agreement anytime before the maturity date, but expect to pay a small penalty for that.

If you are more adventurous, you can set up a fixed deposit in a currency other than your own, but then you will be moving out on the risk curve. Many banks will arrange a so-called carry trade for you, where you for instance borrow in Japanese Yen at 0.5% and invest the money in USD at 3%, scoring the difference in the process. The real bold investors might consider the Mexican Peso at 11% p.a.; after bank charges that would give you 10% p.a. Easy return, right? What could possibly go wrong? A drop in value of the invested currency – that's what could go wrong. There is usually a reason why that other country pays such an "attractive" return, and that reason is more often than not an unsustainable macroeconomic regime that sooner or later will result in currency devaluation.

Here is a case story from real life. While I was working in the oil patch in the early 1980s, some of my expat colleagues loved going from Singapore to Bali for R&R during their time off in between field assignments on the rigs. Along the main streets near the airport and along Kuta Beach, there were plenty of money changer shops, who would also take deposits; some of my friends saw that the deposit interest rate on the Indonesian Rupiah (IDR) was 15–16% p.a. and jumped in, converting and depositing their fat USD pay checks to get this generous return.

I cannot say I haven't made mistakes in my financial journey, but I can guarantee you that I didn't fall for that one. At that time, you got around 700 IDR for each USD; but trade deficits, falling foreign reserves and local inflation in Indonesia meant the IDR value was sliding. I didn't trust those fly-by-night Balinese money changers one bit anyway. Then overnight, 30 March 1983, the Indonesian central bank devalued the IDR to 970 to the USD; by then the currency had dropped 38% in a year! But that wasn't enough, the Rupiah kept sliding, and on 12 September 1986 it was devalued another 30%; that day the exchange rate was set at 1,664 IDR to the US Dollar. Instead of scoring a windfall, by that time my friends had lost half their hard-earned money. During the Asian Financial Crisis in 1997, the IDR fell further to 7,900 and it has never really recovered from that. Today when I checked, the rate to the USD was 14,673. Maybe currency speculation is not for everyone, and it certainly isn't for the faint-hearted.

So if we leave the currency issue aside, moving on from fixed deposit, in the securities industry there are basically two types of products: bonds and shares. If you buy a bond, you are a "loaner"; if you buy a share, you are an "owner".

A bond is a debt obligation issued by a government or a private company in the credit market; it is a loan that will be paid back to the buyer of the bond, the investor, over a specified period of time, typically anywhere from two years to 30. The bond pays the investor interest; it has a coupon rate that is fixed for the duration of the loan, i.e. until maturity, when the principal will the returned to the investor. That is why the bond market is often referred to as "fixed income". While the coupon rate is fixed, the yield is not. In the secondary market, the price of the bond will fluctuate according to supply and demand. If, for instance, a $100 bond has a coupon payment of $2 per year, the yield is 2% p.a. That is OK if the prevailing interest rate is 2%, but should it go up to 4%, the investor will only pay $50 for the bond, as by paying only $50, the annual yield goes up to 2/50 = 4%. That was what happened in 2022 and 2023: when the interest rates worldwide were increased to fight inflation, bond prices came down – to the point where some banks, such as Silicon Valley Bank in California, who were holding a lot of their reserves in bonds, became insolvent and eventually bankrupt.

In spite of this, bonds are considered a lower-risk investment than shares – we will get to shares in a moment. Bond-holders always have the option of holding on to their bonds, and although the yield/return might drop for a while, they will get their money back at maturity. That is, if the bond issuer can pay! While government bonds in general are considered risk-free, company bonds are definitely not. Even apparently good companies can surprise on the downside and default on their loan obligations. To guide investors, credit rating agencies assign a credit rating to each bond. Roughly there are two categories: investment grade bonds, rated between AAA (highest rating) and BBB (adequate), and then speculative bonds, usually referred to charmingly as "junk bonds", which have ratings from BB down the scale to D (for default!).

Most countries give small investors easy access to government debt. In the past you could buy government bonds of various issuances, coupon rates and maturities at the local post office. In Singapore these days, you can buy Singapore Saving Bonds (SSBs) at the nearest ATM machine if you have an account with one of the three major banks and a CDP account operated by SGX, the Singapore Exchange. All Singapore government debt is rated AAA (Triple A). The minimum investment is only S$500; the maximum for individuals is S$200,000. The effective rate at the moment is 3.07% p.a. but will obviously vary; check the internet for the current effective rate. All other countries I know of have a similar government-sponsored investment scheme, although not all are AAA-rated, of course – in some countries, government debt is rated junk! The interest on a short-term government bond is the closest thing you get to the so-called risk-free rate of return, a somewhat theoretical number used in financial analysis as the base case for a risk-free investment.

Private credit is a bit different. To finance their operations, most companies issue bonds in larger denominations, starting at $5,000 and often at $100,000 or even $200,000. As such, buying individual bonds is mainly for wealthy individuals or for institutional investors such as pension funds. For smaller private investors who need to spread their risk, I would advise buying into a bond fund to get exposure to the private credit market.

Collective investment schemes offer many opportunities for investing in the bond market, which is colossal, worth over US$100 trillion worldwide. In the US alone, the bond market at around $40 trillion in value is double the size of the equity market. Through banks and internet trading platforms, small investors can access either mutual funds or ETFs (Exchange-Traded Funds) linked to bonds. While mutual funds are open-ended funds valued only once a day at the end of trading, ETFs have become popular in recent years because they have a fixed number of shares that are traded all trading day, just like stocks, by the minute. Since ETFs in general track an underlying basket of securities or commodities, they are passively managed and have low annual expense ratios (below 1%, with some as low as 0.15–0.20% p.a.), while trading fees and annual expense ratios are typically higher for mutual funds that are more actively managed by a team of analysts selecting and trading suitable securities. Bond funds can give you exposure to a variety of bonds, both government and private, and at various degrees of risk level, from investment grade to "high yield" – which is a nicer term for junk bonds. As always, the higher the risk, the greater is the potential for reward, as well as failure. Since bond funds hold a basket of different securities, should one of them go bust, it is not the end of the world; some junk bond funds have an expected yearly default rate of 2–4%, but the much higher rate of return on the rest is supposed to counter this risk.

For many years, nominal interest rates were so low that fixed income was a miserable place to park your money. With a slight increase in central bank funds rates in the US, EU and associated countries since 2022, bond investments might prove more attractive going forward, considering their supposedly "safe", low-risk, structure. At the end of this chapter, when we look at asset class allocation, we will consider how they can be part of your investment portfolio.

A BIT MORE ABOUT SHARES

So, if you buy a share, a stock, you become an "owner"; publicly listed companies with limited liability form the backbone of our capitalist economic structure. Of course, many important companies around the world are *not* listed; their shares are privately held and not traded on any public exchange. As a case in point, I found it amusing watching Shou Zi Chew being interrogated by members of the US Congress in March 2023; at the time, the government was considering banning TikTok in the US due to its close links with its Chinese-owned parent company ByteDance and supposedly the Chinese Communist Party. As CEO of TikTok, Mr Chew was questioned aggressively by numerous members of Congress who time and again asked about how much money TikTok made in America and other financial details. I thought Chew (who is actually a Singaporean) handled himself well under tremendous pressure in a hostile environment, and it was especially revealing when Chew was able to brush off every question about TikTok's finances, by politely reiterating that he was not able or obliged to answer questions of that nature. As a privately held company, TikTok in America does not have to disclose its financial details. When Mark Zuckerberg appears before Congress, as he regularly does, he does not have that privilege, though; his company, Meta Platforms (=Facebook), is publicly listed and traded and must publish quarterly reports as well as annual reports detailing all its financial transactions for the benefit of investors and the public at large.

Of course, as an investor you can buy into a privately owned company, if you can team up with the founders and come to an agreement. However, an investment like that in the "private equity" space is not liquid and is usually reserved for high-net-worth individuals and institutional investors. Alternatively, if you start your own firm, as sole proprietor you would usually be liable for any claims on the firm with all your assets. If you buy shares in a publicly listed company, however, you only risk the money you put in; that is why the arrangement is called "limited' – yes, the company can go belly-up and you might lose your whole invest-ment, but creditors can never come after you and force you to cough up additional funds.

So, to simplify matters a bit here, let us stick to publicly traded share investments, as there is already plenty to consider in this segment. First of all, how do you value the shares of a company? You don't want to pay too much for them, right? How do you determine if that company might make a good investment going forward? Well, unfortunately in finance we only have the past to look back on, but based on the past, as well as our somewhat subjective opinion about the future, we can develop an opinion. Those who scrutinize the past and extrapolate from there are called *technical analysts*; they are inclined to believe that history tends to repeat itself, so they draw graphs and charts and look for "head and shoulder" patterns, watch when the moving 50-day average breaks out and crosses the 200-day moving average from below (a signal to buy), study trading volume and momen-tum indicators – all for the purpose of judging whether to buy or sell a certain stock. I have friends who think that technical analysis is mumbo jumbo, and I have others who think that there might be some validity to it, especially for short-term traders who are looking for the right timing to get in and out of the market.

Most analysts, however, agree that to gauge the value of a stock, a solid fundamental analysis is required. Virtually all the infor-mation about a company that you will need is available online today, but if you find the information overwhelming, just focus on a few metrics. The P/E ratio is widely used; it is the current price of the stock divided by the latest published earnings. Say stock

A is trading at $20 and the earnings per share were $2; the P/E would be 10. This is an indication of how many years it will take you to make your investment back, so it is also referred to as the "multiple". Of course, the company will usually not pay out all its earnings to shareholders every year, but even if it retains most of its earnings and reinvests them in new projects or in share buy-backs, this should add to the value of the company and eventually to your overall return, which is income from dividends plus profit from share price increases. It would be reasonable to expect the company to pay around half its earnings as dividends; if company A does that, you would receive $1 in dividends and your dividend yield would be 1/20 = 5% p.a.

One consideration now is that while dividend payments in many countries are taxed as income, capital gains for overseas investors are not. In the US, companies withhold 30% in tax at source on behalf of the federal government, and for investors abroad, this tax is virtually impossible to recover, even if you as a non-resident are not liable for taxation. Dividend income from my Danish investments is taxed at 27%, in Norway it is 15%; you are unlikely to ever see this money again. I guess the NATO countries need it for their foreign wars, so there is little we small overseas investors can do about it, although it eats into our overall return. It might be of some consolation to those of you who live in the Free World, outside of EU and NATO control, that the locals end up paying a *lot* more than the 30% withholding tax on their dividends, as the dividend income is added to other income, so the marginal tax rate might be 40% or even 50%. That is one of many reasons I prefer to invest most of my assets in Singapore, where there is no tax on dividend income; here we don't waste money by waging war against others.

There are many other metrics you can use in fundamental share analysis, but let us stick to the P/E ratio for now to simplify things. So-called *value investors* look for established blue-chip companies with good fundamentals, competitive advantage, and preferably a high barrier to entry and strong pricing power. They prefer steady earnings, generous dividend payments, little or no debt, high book-to-price ratio and low P/E. Obviously a low P/E ratio would be better than a high one, but things are not always so straightforward. For many years in the early 2000s, the P/E ratio for Amazon.com Inc was some 200, i.e. astronomical; for the first many years, the company had negative earnings, so the ratio couldn't even be calculated in a meaningful manner. Yet, while the company was worth $10.2 billion in 2003, 20 years later it was worth 100 times that, over $1 trillion. Patient investors with nerves of steel were richly rewarded and traditionalists looking only at fundamentals lost out. The same story goes for Facebook, Tesla and the other tech stock darlings, many of which shot up further in value during the Covid-19 lockdowns of 2020–21 when technology became king and early investors laughed all the way to the bank.

IT'S A RISKY BUSINESS

So, are you a value investor or growth enthusiast? The battle between the two is not quite over, and probably never will be. Either way, once you develop an opinion about a company that you like, you have to understand that there are two types of risk in the stock investment field. There is the *specific risk* that your company is under: Due to internal management problems or market conditions specific to that company or market segment, the company could falter and its shares could turn south. That happens all the time whenever a company hits some headwinds and comes out with bad annual results that disappoint market observers. The other risk is *systemic risk*, or *market risk*; that is when the whole system goes hay-wire and the markets crash. That could be due to macroeconomic conditions such as rapidly rising interest rates and/or inflation or a recession; but it could also be because of Black Swan events like war, terrorist attacks or natural disasters.

It is important for investors to accept that there is little you can do to mitigate systemic risk. In a time like that, we all take it on the chin and go down together. You just have to wait it out; but try to keep some "dry powder" in reserve, i.e. cash that you can put to work in the market when you are convinced that the hard times are coming to an end and all the bad news has been priced into stocks. Experience shows that when that happens, markets will recover, sometimes pretty quickly.

You can guard against specific risk by diversifying your portfolio. Surveys have shown that just holding two or three different stocks will reduce your risk substantially; many analysts recommend that you buy into some 30 different companies over time, preferably in different sectors with low correlation and maybe even in different countries and currencies.

If you are not comfortable picking individual stocks yourself, maybe you are better off buying into a mutual fund or ETF holding a basket of stocks. As we saw under the fixed income section, mutual funds and ETFs typically invest in a large basket of securities. That might be a good instrument for you, if you for instance want to bet on the tech industry going forward, a strategy that it might be hard to argue with, the way things look now. Many start-ups and even some tech giants will falter and fail, but most analysts seem to agree that the sector as a whole has a bright future. The same might be said for sectors like healthcare, financials and energy – all important sectors with time on their side. But which company will make it big, which will fail miserably? That is not easy to predict. So instead of worrying about individual names, find an ETF tracking the sector you like and go for it – you will sleep better at night that way.

If you really want to reduce your specific risk down to almost nothing, you can look at index funds; then you only have the market risk to worry about, and that risk can never be completely eliminated. In the US, the S&P 500 index monitors 500 different companies, as the name says, and is probably the most popular gauge for overall market performance. Warren Buffett, the most quoted tycoon of all, recommends investors to simply buy into the S&P 500 and hold "forever".

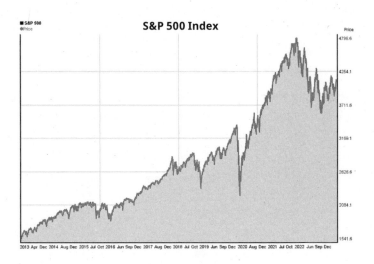

Indeed, looking at the graph, in spite of a bad 20% dip when Covid-19 hit in 2020, the stock market has done quite well during the last 10 years. Not counting some local developments, charts for most jurisdictions' stock markets would have a similar shape. Overall, since the S&P 500 attained its current structure in 1957, the market has produced an average annual compounded return of 10.15%.[39] That is why you shouldn't keep your money under the mattress!

AND WHAT ABOUT SUSTAINABILITY?

But what about the sustainability of all this? Can our current trajectory go on forever? No, in my view, and many others', it cannot, that is all there is to it. Our economic model is designed to extract natural capital and convert it into financial capital – more and more of it, we can never get enough. But we can run out of easy resources to pick. Like the gold miner I mentioned before, on virgin ground in some never-before-explored mountain stream, he starts by picking up the exposed gold nuggets on top of the gravel first, and then it gets gradually harder from there to find and extract the rest of the metal. You pick the low-hanging fruit first, and then you climb up into the tree and out onto the thin branches, until they break and you come down to earth. In industry, we have picked all the easy fruits long ago. In the early oil fields in west Texas and later Ghawar, Saudi Arabia, you extracted 100 barrels of oil for each one you used (EROI = 100). Today some thermally enhanced oil recovery fields yield as little as 2 EROI, according to one study.[40] You use one barrel and get two back. It's hardly worth it.

But aren't all investments supposed to be sustainable? If your investment cannot be sustained, shouldn't you put your money somewhere else? We investors first of all really just have to get a return on our capital now; otherwise we won't be investors for very much longer – there will be nothing to invest. We need to protect our savings, future-proof them and make them grow. And there are tool you can apply to make your investments more sustainable, or at least less exposed to the risk of collapse. On top of that, if you are really concerned about the sustainability of our situation, the good news is that just as we have converted natural capital to financial capital for years, decades and probably centuries, the reverse can also happen! Just like water can be turned into steam and back into a liquid, money in the bank can be made into thriving wetlands and rich forests! We will look at that a little bit later in Chapter 7.

Enter SRI, ESG, CSR and all the other acronyms. Let me provide a simple taxonomy of the key terms in sustainable investing.

If you notice on the chart below, as you move down the list, the focus on profitability gradually diminishes until you finally simply just give your money away. CSR is the weakest case for sustainability; even coal mining giants, logging companies and weapons manufacturers will try to do their bit by having fair HR practices and take their staff for birdwatching trips and coastal clean-up exercises. The fact that their everyday operations are wrecking the Earth big-time doesn't really play into this. Then comes the ESG concept, at the moment the most widely used term in sustainable investment circles. Since it consists of three quite different focus areas, not every company will have the same priorities. Some will be more concerned about lessening environmental impact while others will focus on ensuring good governance in the organization.

Investing Terminology
(in increasing order of impact focus)

Term	Meaning	Goal
Conventional	Conventional Investing	Maximize financial return
CSR	Corporate Social Responsibility	Maximize financial return; but with consideration to staff, other stake-holders and society at large; also called "good corporate citizenship"
SRI	Socially Responsible Investing	Maximize returns with politically correct and socially responsible strategies
ESG	Environmental, Social and Governance	Three-pronged approach to max-imize returns while considering environmental and social standards
Sustainable	Sustainable Investing	Used synonymously with ESG, but with emphasis on the "E"
Ethical	Ethical Investing	Generate financial returns while applying your ethical values to investment decisions
Impact	Impact Investing	Generate some returns while having a positive impact on soci-ety in general
Philanthropy	Charity	Donate money to good causes to promote welfare for others or for the environment

Ethical Investing? Hey, I wrote a whole book about this, so I think I have done my part to popularize the topic! A truly ethical investor may be willing to forgo a bit of extra Alpha (finance slang for excess return) by screening out (i.e. avoiding in her portfolio) some companies that she might find unethical, e.g. "sin stocks" like gambling, tobacco, booze or nuclear weapons. Instead, that person might actively select ethically "good" companies involved in "green" energy, organic farming, healthcare or fair-trade products.

Next down the list is Impact Investing, which usually refers to private equity investors starting community businesses that have a direct local social impact such as providing employment opportunities for minority groups or ex-convicts, as well as cleaning up the neighbourhood or running recycling or re-use enterprises. For impact investors, the profit, although nice to have, is optional. So that is just before the stage where the wealthy individual simply gives her money away in pure philanthropy, to people or volunteer societies that need it more than her.

There is no doubt that ESG investing, to use the most widely accepted term for this trend, is here to stay and growing rapidly. In a recent study by Harvard Law School, the researchers expect ESG managed funds to increase worldwide from 14.4% of Assets under Management (AUM) in 2021 to 21.5% in 2026.[41] In the US alone, the AUM in numbers under ESG management are expected to increase from $4.5 trillion to $10.5 trillion, partly pushed by government legislation to promote "green growth". A 2022 survey by Capital Group found that 89% of investors consider ESG issues "in some form" as part of their investment approach; a similar percentage of public companies, 88%, have

ESG initiatives in place; for private companies, the percentage is somewhat smaller, around 66%.[42]

With this remarkable shift in investor strategies and priorities having taken place within a few years, not even decades, two things come to my mind:

1. Investors now increasingly see their money management in its totality; it has become a lifestyle. Yes, everyone wants good ROI, but with so many financial products now available and online trading platforms where you can execute your own trades on a daily basis at very little cost, investing has become more and more like a leisure activity, as shopping used to be, if you will. So just like with shopping, there are multiple benefits: not just the cost/benefit, price versus utility, but also the social outcome and the personal satisfaction of the whole exercise. You buy into a listed company that you can relate to. You might, for instance, buy a Tesla car because you admire Elon Musk; now you might buy Tesla stock for the same reason. You like Apple products, so you buy Apple stock as well. You hate Bill Gates with a vengeance, so you short Microsoft (you can use options or Contract for Difference CFDs to do that, but I will not get into derivative trading here) and laugh your head off when you cash in on a decline in his stock. Trading and investing have become a way of expressing yourself, of making a bit of difference, gaining a bit of influence; you put your money where your mouth is.

2. With such a large proportion of AUM in the finance industry flowing into sustainable investments of some sort, the segment is increasingly losing its edge. Although regulators, stock exchanges and other capital market participants have tried to set some standards, we still don't have clear, concise, unambiguous definitions and criteria for what constitutes a "sustainable" investment, a "green" bond or a "socially responsible" company. The quotation marks are there for a reason! The field is wide open for greenwashing, manipulation, dishonesty and borderline fraud. If you don't believe me, read "Greenwashing is becoming a big problem for ESG" on Techwireasia.com.[43] On a positive note, the story also says that in 2023, MAS (Singapore's central bank) will start issuing guidelines for ESG funds marketed to retail investors here; maybe there is hope for some clarity in the future.

MANAGING THE PORTFOLIO

So, there you have it. For getting a better return on your money than cash or fixed deposit, you have your choice of fixed income products or shares. For shares, you might consider either identifying individual companies you like and believe in, or you can take the safer option and invest in a large basket of companies through a fund or an index ETF. There are ETFs for every taste these days, for every sector of the market and even for properties, commodities and alternative investments.

If you are concerned about sustainability, financial or environmental, there is a product for you too. In fact, there are many out there, thousands. Each single fund provider and CMS licence holder will offer you SRI/ESG/Sustainable products of various configurations. But open up the hood and have a look at the engine before you buy, see what exactly is in this selection of companies. You might be surprised. Many sustainable funds are packed with technology companies and even materials, pharmaceuticals and banks that you might not be so happy to be associated with.

Consider the case of Nestlé. "Whenever there is a discussion about the most corrupt and unethical corporations in the world," one source asserts, "Nestlé always tops the list."[44] Nestlé, it would seem, does not tick *any* of the three ESG boxes: It extracts free groundwater and sells it back to poor people at an exorbitant mark-up; its plastic bottles then pollute the environment; it uses unpaid child labour in its chocolate business; and it pushes baby formula milk on uneducated mothers who would be better off breast-feeding – the rural women mix the formula with too much or contaminated water, resulting in thousands of infant deaths. And yet I have seen Nestle S.A. on the list of companies in a sustainability fund offered by a Danish bank I deal with; I suppose the nice profits from Nestlé lift the performance of the fund, never mind the ethics of it. I am sure you can find similar horror stories yourself if you try.

Finally, you have to consider the proportional allocation of your assets. The classical asset allocation is the 60:40 portfolio, meaning 60% in fixed income and 40% in stocks. But this can be tweaked in an infinite number of ways. In *Be Financially Free*, I recommended considering a Gone Fishin' Portfolio, developed by American investment strategist Alexander Green. So it is interesting now, some seven years later, to see how this allocation has performed. The proportion in a Gone Fishin' Portfolio is roughly 60:40 reversed: 60% stocks, and 40% bonds and others. More precisely:

- 15% US Stocks
- 15% US Small Cap Stocks
- 10% European Stocks
- 10% Pacific Stocks
- 10% Emerging Markets Stocks
- 10% Short-Term Investment-Grade Bonds
- 10% High-Yield Corporate Bonds
- 10% TIPS (Treasury Inflation-Protected Securities)
- 5% REITs
- 5% Precious Metals

REITs are Real Estate Investment Trusts, i.e. a collective property investment vehicle. The fact that it is a trust (and not a property company) means that there are some restrictions on how much debt the trust can take on, and as much as 90% of earnings have to be returned to shareholders as dividends, so REITs are favoured by investors looking for a steady stream of income, rather than spectacular gains in share price.

This allocation is somewhat US-centric, but you could easily tweak it to fit the country you are in. In 2023, an independent financial analyst had a look at Green's work and concluded that yes, the Gone Fishin' Portfolio had indeed gone up nicely during the past 10 years. Had you invested $10,000 in this way in 2010, by 2021 you would have had $23,000. However, had you invested in the S&P 500 index during the same period, your capital would have grown to $42,000.

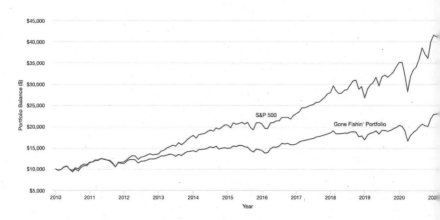

It is worth noting, though, that on a risk-adjusted basis, the difference would be smaller. Green's portfolio had a standard deviation over the period of 11.28% versus 13.98% for the index, indicating a lower risk.[45] In finance, the standard deviation is used as the denominator in the Sharpe ratio, which is a measurement of risk-adjusted return where the numerator is portfolio performance minus the prevailing risk-free interest rate, i.e. your Alpha. So a low standard deviation (which is the square root of the average variance) gives a higher Sharpe ratio and this is considered favourable. In other words, you can sleep sounder at night with a Gone Fishin' Portfolio; over a longer period, from 2001 to 2021, the two moved very closely in lockstep, but again with lower risk for Green's combination of financial instruments. Green advises that you tweak your investments once a year. Each January you adjust the allocation percentages back, by selling a bit of what did well, and buying what did poorly the previous year. This should take about 20 minutes according to Green. The rest of the year you go back to fishing or whatever you enjoy doing – a strategy that sounds pretty good to me!

In *Be Financially Free*, I also looked at one of the big players in the investment field: GIC Pte Ltd, previously the Government of Singapore Investment Corporation, which manages most of the country's nest egg, in particular the compulsory pension funds. GIC only invests abroad, and to spread their risk and improve performance, they diversify into various asset classes. Let us look at how GIC has tweaked the allocation since seven years ago:

Percentage allocation 2016 vs. 2022:

- Developed Market Equities: 29% reduced to 14%
- Emerging Market Equities: 18% reduced to 16%
- Private Equity: 9% increased to 17%
- Real Estate: 7% increased to 10%
- Nominal Bonds and Cash: 32% increased to 37%
- Inflation-linked Bonds: 5% increased to 6%

So as of March 2022, GIC had about 47% of their assets in stocks, listed or privately held, down a bit from previous years. If you add the real estate investments to stocks, you have about 57% in hard assets and the other 43% in fixed income and cash instruments. The 60:40 portfolio is not that popular after all among the big players; they all seem to have an overweight in stocks – and, I suspect, so should you.

Performance-wise, GIC cannot beat the S&P 500 index benchmark either, but they are not doing too badly. According to their website: "Over the 20-year period that ended 31 March 2022, GIC achieved an annualized return of 4.2% above global inflation."[M6] If you can do the same, I would say you are doing alright.

So to rub in my sustainability message, let me show you one final interesting chart.

It links back to the previous chapter and shows two things. First of all, the explosive growth in productivity and wealth since the Great Acceleration started around 1950 (here for the US; most countries would display the same pattern). But it also shows something else. Less and less of this wealth is being captured by the working people – the disconnect started in the early 1970s and has not really been fixed since. Where did the rest of the productivity increase go? It has been captured by capital! So don't rely on your salary alone; collect a share of the return on capital out there. Will this trend continue? We don't know the future, but there are some signs that the previous decades of high return on capital will be harder to achieve going forward; it might not be sustainable. We will look at that in the next chapter.

5

Can You Make Money, Sustainably?

TRADING VERSUS INVESTING

Before we look at the profitability of sustainable investing, let us wrap up the loose ends covering your asset allocation preferences. As we saw with the very conservative strategies, such as the Gone Fishin' Portfolio, the GIC 57:43 equity/debt ratio and the old Buffett mantra of just buying and holding an ETF tracking the S&P 500 index, these approaches don't leave much room for manoeuvrability. I can understand if younger investors would want a little more control and excitement in their lives.

It is important to understand that while I, and most other traditional analysts, recommend that you diversify your investments, by diversifying you might also forgo rapid and explosive gains. The world of finance is full of success stories like Peter Lim, currently the 16th richest person in Singapore. Lim didn't diversify or buy the index; in the 1990s he poured everything he had, some US$10 million, into Wilmar International Ltd, a palm oil start-up.[47] Some years later, in 2010, he sold his share for $1.5 billion and went out to buy Liverpool FC. Right, Liverpool didn't want him, so he bought Valencia CF of Spain instead, but the point is that with his tactics, Peter Lim made himself into a billionaire investor and philanthropist. So as an inspiration for all young people, the message from Peter Lim's story is: Don't diversify! Forget about sustainability. Pile all your money into one single promising start-up and ignore issues such as habitat conservation and protecting the rainforest; that way you will be successful beyond your wildest dreams!

Technology has made it easier for newbie investors to pursue this get-rich-quick dream. When I started buying shares in the 1970s and 80s, you needed a licensed broker to do the trades for you over the phone. Then you had to go to his office and collect the actual paper shares, nicely decorated physical documents with the correct denominations. To sell, you had to make another trip, bringing the papers to the broker's office, and each time your broker would charge you about 1% in transaction fees. We didn't think that it could ever be any different.

But of course today it is. You can do your own trading from your home computer or your phone, and commissions are as low as 0.2% or even 0.08% per transaction. Some trading platforms offer 0% commission charges, but that doesn't mean that their services are free; it just means that the platform makes money by selling your orders to a third party, who will make a buck on the bid/offer spread.

Young people can get caught up in this, such as day trading, where you try to wrap up and go back to cash after each trading day (or trading night, if you are into the overseas markets). Or using derivatives like options and futures to speed up and gear your investments by a factor of 10 or more. That latter tactic will obviously increase potential gains, but also potential losses. Some traders will outperform the market like that, but it is a sad fact that most do not; they just end up feeding the system and the middlemen making money from all this "churning", as it is called. In that way, stock and options trading resembles gambling, where only one thing is certain: Due to the concept of Gambler's Ruin, it is a statistical certainty that if you keep playing a 50-50 game against someone with infinite funds, you will always lose all your money. As they say, "The house always wins" – it is actually true. You can look it up if you want to see the interesting math behind this phenomenon.

I also don't really believe that young workers should take on more risk than older people. It is standard advice in finance that your relative allocation of shares in your portfolio should be 100 minus your age. So if you start investing as a 20-year-old, keep 80% of your capital in shares and the rest in fixed income. By the time you turn centenarian with a bit of luck, all your money should be in bonds. That may be so, but as a general rule, I don't believe young people can afford to lose their money more than older ones can. Young people should protect and future-proof their savings just as well as mature people should. Right, in theory, you can better afford to take a hit if you are young, as you will have more years to make up for the losses. But why take a hit at all? That doesn't really make sense to me.

Surveys have shown that Millennials (Gen Y, born 1981–96) and even Gen Z (1997–2012) have a high propensity for getting into new risky financial instruments such as cryptocurrencies. I am no expert on this, so I will leave the crypto space alone for now; I found *The End of Money: The story of bitcoin, cryptocurrencies and the blockchain revolution* (Rothstein, 2017) very enlightening to read, but this is such a fast-evolving field that the status of the various digital "currencies", if that is what they are (I doubt that most digital coins, if any, would qualify for the term "currency"), change by the month and the week. I know, some people made billions developing and trading in digital assets, and it is tempting for the tech-savvy to have a go at it as well. I just can't help you there. I hear about the evil "rug-pull" schemes where scammers introduce a new digital coin or NFT, get influencers to talk the price up and then sell out and disappear with the cash. In that way, there is nothing new under the sun: we have had Ponzi schemes and "pump and dump" manipulation (a rug-pull with a small-cap speculative stock) for generations.

I am sometimes asked by young investors: "Should I buy Bitcoin?" And then I don't know what to say. I advised against that when Bitcoin was $200 and now it is $30,000; so much for my expert advice. Buy if you must, and provided no one steals it from your digital wallet, maybe it will go to $100,000, maybe a million, as some people claim. But if I were you, I would only put in as much money as I could afford to lose, maybe 5% of my net worth, because chances are pretty good that is exactly what will happen: you could lose it all.

So I will wrap this up quickly with a quote from one of the finance professionals that I respect. At a panel discussion at the 2023

Davos World Economic Forum, Singapore's then Senior Minister Tharman Shanmugaratnam, who was also chairman of the Monetary Authority of Singapore, was asked if cryptocurrencies shouldn't be better regulated. Other panel members, such as the Bank of France governor, predictably enough for an EU bureaucrat, called for more regulation and legislation. But Mr Tharman said instead, that while it was "very clear" that the cryptocurrency space has to be regulated for things like money laundering, "dabbling in cryptocurrency is a foolish risk taken at one's own expense". So when it comes to regulating cryptocurrency the same way as banks and insurance companies for financial stability reasons, there is a need to take a step back and ask a basic philosophical question: "Does that legitimize something that's inherently purely speculative? And in fact, slightly crazy? Or are we better off just providing ultra clarity as to what's an unregulated market and if you go in, you go in at your own risk. I lean a bit more towards the latter view."[48] For what it is worth, so do I!

CAN OR NOT?

So can you make money in sustainable, SRI, ESG, ethical investing, call it what you want? In *Your Essential Guide to Sustainable Investing* (2022), authors Swedroe and Adams put a lot of effort into trying to answer that question. Their reply is a resounding yes: you *can* make money with a strategy considering sustainability. But when it comes to the most important matter – Do you make more or less than investing conventionally – the case is not quite as clear. What the average investor would like to know is: Will it cost me to invest in sustainability, or can I beat the market doing it?

Swedroe and Adams conclude that investing with sustainability in mind is not that much different from conventional investing. As we saw in the previous chapter, today a majority of investors, especially institutional investors and professional money managers, claim to apply or at least consider ESG matters in decision-making. The authors say that "ESG investing now accounts for one of three dollars under professional management in the US, but one of every two dollars in Europe". The finance industry is a huge and important sector, so with the quite recent explosive growth in the sustainability field, many surveys published in distinguished finance journals such as *The Journal of Impact and ESG Investing* have investigated the profitability issue.

The Government Pension Fund of Norway, which has well over $1 trillion in capital and is one of the largest sovereign wealth funds in the world, has a sustainability policy and screens out certain businesses from its portfolio such as tobacco companies, thermal coal and weapons manufacturers. The fund has grown nicely through the years, thank you, but when the fund conducted their own investigation in 2017, they found that their exclusion policy had cost them. Over the previous 11 years, by screening out especially the tobacco companies and some nuclear arms manufacturers, the fund had missed out on 1.1 percentage points of cumulative gains. So, their ethics had a price, but the Norwegians accepted this. Somehow it seems logical when Swedroe and Adams conclude that "sustainable investors sacrifice some of the benefits of diversification relative to a broad-based market index fund".

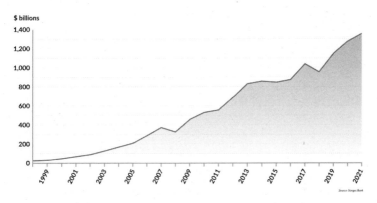

Norway's Government Pension Fund market value over the past 20+ years. In spite of forgoing additional potential gains from some excluded companies, the fund has done quite nicely.

But that is not the whole story. Swedroe and Adams also quote a 2020 survey on "Carbon Risk" covering 1,600 companies with data from four major ESG databases. The survey identifies two categories of firms, the "brown" and the "green", based on their ESG status and compliance. The authors conclude: "Firms are becoming greener. Over the full period (2010–2016) brown firms performed worse than green firms on average. The cumulative difference in returns between brown and green firms was roughly 14 percent, with green firms outperforming."

Swedroe and Adams make an important observation: "Economic theory suggests that if a large enough proportion of investors choose to favor companies with high sustainability ratings and avoid those with low sustainability ratings (sin businesses), the favored company's share prices will be elevated and the sin shares will be depressed." This is important, because "the result is that the favored companies will have a lower cost of capital because they will trade at a higher P/E ratio." The lower cost of capital means that the company can borrow cheaper and issue additional shares in rights issues at better prices. But the authors also point out: "The flip side of the lower cost of capital is a lower return to the providers of that capital (shareholders)."

This may explain why ESG funds and ETFs have done well in the last few years. In *Sustainable Investing* (2022), the authors conclude that "sustainable indices don't suffer from a performance disadvantage... Recent research suggests that sustainable funds may receive a slightly higher return than traditional funds." However, if you look closer at why that is, it is because increased demand for companies with "green" credentials has pushed up prices. So investors have benefited from capital gains, not so much from profits. That means that if earnings don't follow suit in the coming years, this advantage could be temporary. As the P/E ratios will be pushed up too, going forward, that means a larger multiple, lower relative earnings and lower return for investors. The "brown" companies, i.e. the "sin stocks", coal and oil companies and such, will have lower prices of shares, but better return on capital for investors.

In his foreword to *Your Essential Guide to Sustainable Investing*, veteran financial analyst Burton Malkiel sums it up this way: "A heightened demand for ESG-compliant investments can cause share prices to rise and thus enhance the return of sustainable funds. [But] any short-term benefits will be realized at the expense of long-term performance." So the bottom line for Malkiel is: "There is no unambiguous evidence that sustainable investing enhances long-term financial performance."

So, there you have it. You can listen to all the advice you want, but at the end of the day you as an investor are on your own. You have to apply your own values and your own judgement. If you are concerned about ethics or sustainability, you can express your views with your capital allocation. I do that, up to a point. Like the Norwegian Oil Fund, I don't buy tobacco and weapons-of-mass-destruction companies, also not gambling stocks. Companies like that ruin people's lives and I don't care how low the P/E ratio goes; let it go to 2, they can keep their profits. I like to make money as much as the next guy, but I am just not that desperate. That is why I don't have any index fund share products either, to avoid the Phillip Morris, the Lockheed Martin and the Las Vegas Sands of the world (all three included in the S&P 500 index). Instead, I buy into the companies I like to be associated with or at least can accept.

I am not always successful in my stock selection, of course. Some picks work out spectacularly, a few have gone just as spectacularly bad. I know that not everyone can accept that kind of risk, but I can. The good news about owning individual names like that is that you don't always have to be right; to make money, you just have to be right 51% of the time and that is perfectly possible. I prefer to buy and hold; some stocks I have had for more than 20 years. I know that there is another school out there: the momentum traders. One of the CNBC commentators is in that camp: Joe Terranova, who wrote *Buy High, Sell Higher: Why Buy-and-Hold is Dead* (2012). Look into it if you want to, but always keep an open mind; and do consider that Terranova's net worth is reported to be $1 million – not really that impressive for a 56-year-old celebrity financial expert.

THE ENERGY TRANSITION

As I have highlighted, we are all different and we all have different priorities. What is important is that we make our own choices and recognize our diversity, without pointing fingers. On my part, as I mentioned, there are some companies I definitely don't want to be connected with, ever. Then there are those I love and who have made me a lot of money over the years in a sustainable manner. And then there are the "maybes". It is like the classic red-green-amber priority system.

In the amber "Maybe" category, you might find the oil companies. I used to work in the business and I loved every minute of it, so I can hardly rule that sector out completely, that would be somewhat hypocritical. I had more oil shares back then; today I only have one, or rather my son (born 2002) has. In 2003, our family, including our 8-month-old, visited Stavanger, Norway, where I used to live myself for a while in the 1970s. While in town, my wife and I walked into Norske Bank (now DNB Bank) and opened a savings account for our son. I put in 100,000 Norwegian Kroner (around US$9,500); the interest rate was 3% p.a. My intention was to leave the money for my son's education – I reckoned the NOK would strengthen in value over time. The next year, the bank lowered the deposit rate to 2%, and when they lowered it again to 1%, I had enough. Our money was rotting in the bank! I bought NOK50,000 worth of DNB Bank stock, figuring that since they were ripping off their customers they would probably make a boatload of money. And then I bought NOK50,000 worth of Statoil stock to spread my risk, all in my son's name (that was possible according to Norwegian legislation).

And what happened? Today, almost 20 years later, my Singaporean son still has that simple portfolio. The NOK didn't appreciate as much as I had expected, but today when I checked, the shares are worth US$50,915. The bank did a lot better over time than the oil company. That valuation does not count annual dividend payments over the period – those have been substantial. I am *so* glad I didn't keep the money in the savings account. My son should start university soon; together with the accumulated dividends, this amount is now enough for him to get a decent degree here in Singapore, where education is heavily subsidized by the state.

Statoil changed its name to Equinor in 2018, and as a shareholder, my son gets the usual invites for an AGM every year. In a letter inviting him for the May 2023 AGM in Stavanger, the announcement included a number of resolutions put forward by other shareholders. One read: "Proposal by shareholder that management of Equinor lets results from global warming determine its future strategy, stops all exploration for oil and gas, phases out production and sale of oil and gas, multiplies its focus on renewable energy and CCS and becomes a climate-friendly company." Of course this resolution didn't pass, but this is shareholder activism in action.

With sustainable investing strategies and ESG policies in place by many, if not most, institutional investors, companies like Equinor are under pressure. Already in 2018, the newspapers could report that many major institutional investors such as churches, universities, pension funds, the City of New York, and at that time the €8.9 billion Ireland Strategic Investment Fund would divest out of fossil fuels, including oil and gas. Irish MP Thomas Pringle said that the wave to sell off all fossil fuel stocks "underlines the necessity of stopping investments in the expansion of a global industry that must be brought to its knees, if catastrophic climate changes are to be avoided".[49]

Brought to its knees? Those are pretty strong words. So let us look at how Statoil/Equinor stock has performed since that statement was made, five years ago:

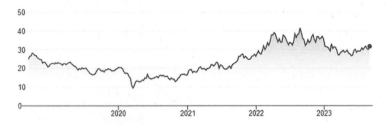

In spite of institutional investors largely boycotting the company, Equinor has done quite alright lately. As Swedroe & Adams (2022) predicted, the somewhat suppressed share price, due to the boycott, has resulted in a low P/E of 10.2 median for the last five years, and a dividend yield of 3.6% over the period, that is, with a 18.7% average payout ratio. Even with such high yield, Equinor retains over 80% of its earnings.[50] By all metrics, it is a really healthy company! What Pringle didn't think of when he threatened to bring Equinor to its knees is that without a drop in demand, the business will continue, even with a higher cost of capital. I am speculating that Pringle probably drove his 4.4L V8 Land Rover to that meeting in Parliament, contributing to that demand; I doubt if he walked all the way.

Although a gigantic organization, with a current market cap of $94 billion, Equinor is but small fry in the oil and gas business. Exxon has a market cap of $448 billion, Chevron is not far behind at $309 billion, and the Saudi Aramco is worth a whopping $2,077 billion.[51]

And the hydrocarbon industry as a whole? There is no sign yet that we will "leave it in the ground", as the greenies claim we should. Depriving the industry of capital might seem like a good idea to some, but the result has so far not been less carbon emitted, just more profits for the energy companies. So the share price goes down a bit? Fine, dividend yield goes up! Investments, exploration of new fields suffer? No problem, the super-low demand elasticity of petroleum products just means that prices go up disproportionately when supply is restricted. We have not been able to hit big oil where it would really hurt: demand.

In *The Ethical Investor's Handbook* (2018), I wrote that the International Energy Agency at that time expected oil production to decline after 2020 from around 80 barrels/day to around 15 barrels/day by 2040: "The IEA says that more electric cars and alternative energy sources 'is enough to keep prices within a $50–70/barrel range to 2040'. Really? Personally I am not so sure about that, but we will see!"

So, now, five years later, let's have a look. I think that the IEA forgot to consider that virtually all the "alternative energy sources", such as solar panels and wind turbines, plus most of the new EVs, are built using fossil energy. Already in October that year, the Brent oil price moved out of the IEA expected trading range to $84/barrel; then after a colossal dip during Covid-19 in 2020 it moved back up to over $80 in January 2021, and peaked at $123/barrel in February 2022 when Russia intervened in the Ukrainian civil war. The price hasn't dropped below $70 since. Could it go back to $30/barrel as it was for a short while during Covid-19? I am sure it could. I am just saying: It is economic growth with high oil prices or recession with low – we can't have it both ways.

What a difference five years can make. First the Covid-19 pandemic and then NATO and Russia at war; in all fairness to IEA, who could have known this would happen back then? Today, most projections for oil look significantly different; the "green transition" has been postponed a bit. Let us look at another more recent projection from the US Energy Information Administration:

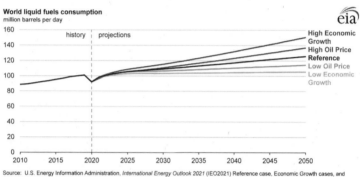

Source: U.S. Energy Information Administration, *International Energy Outlook 2021* (IEO2021) Reference case, Economic Growth cases, and Oil price cases

Yes, the kink in the curve from production cuts in 2020 due to decrease in demand from the Covid-19 pandemic is still there, but otherwise the death of oil appears slightly exaggerated. In the report, the agency says: "To meet the anticipated growth in liquid fuels consumption in the Reference case, we expect a steady increase in crude oil and lease condensate production throughout the projection period. Crude oil is the primary raw material used in the petroleum refining process, and it is a necessary precursor for many finished petroleum products (for example, gasoline, diesel, fuel oil) demanded by all sectors of the economy. To meet increasing demand, countries will need to rely on increased exploration (to identify additional resources), increased drilling (to harvest new and proven reserves), and technology advances (to achieve greater production yields)."[52]

However, as we know, in futuristic projections there is usually a counter-proposal, an alternative view. BP (market cap $110 billion) sticks to the decline-in-oil production outlook in this report:[53]

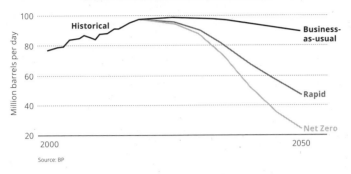

Global oil demand in three scenarios

Source: BP

In 2020, BP staff did their own calculations and compared them to data from the International Energy Agency, considering different scenarios. In the "net zero" case, by 2050 demand for oil will drop to close to 20 million barrels/day. I hope I am still around by then, to check if that will indeed be the case. "Net zero" – there is the term again. Except, no one knows what that means. It has got something to do with offsetting your carbon emissions, but as we will see in the next chapter, there simply aren't enough "green" projects to offset all the hydrocarbon consumption in the world.

I have again, like I did in my two previous finance books, dwelled at some length on our energy situation, carbon-based or otherwise. That is because our development and our entire prosperity since the first Industrial Revolution around 1750, and especially so during the Great Acceleration after 1950, has been completely linked to fossil fuel use, first coal and then oil and gas. Ian Angus uses the phrase "fossil capitalism" for our whole economic structure.

But what about wood? Wood is a sustainable fuel, right? You burn a tree, plant another one, it absorbs carbon while it grows and then you burn it again, what is wrong with that? The problem, again, is the scale. We burn the wood too fast for it to grow back.

A participant in the *Planet of the Humans* documentary, which I referred to earlier, states that you would have to burn *all* the forests of the US to generate enough power to run the grid in the country for one year. And then what? What would you do for the next 50 years while waiting for the forests to grow back? In 2020, Blackrock, the largest asset manager in the world, tried to do the politically correct thing and divest out of coal in the UK. "Climate change has become a defining factor in companies' long-term prospects," Blackrock CEO Larry Fink wrote in a letter to corporate executives. "Awareness is rapidly changing, and I believe we are on the edge of a fundamental reshaping of finance." Instead of coal, Blackrock would keep their 5% stake in UK-based Drax Group PLC, operator of the world's largest wood-burning power plant. There was just one problem. An open letter from 32 environmental organizations from 17 countries urged BlackRock to divest from Drax:[54] "Drax is really the poster child for everything that is wrong with the wood-pellet industry and the wood-based biomass sector." In one year, the UK power plant burned a staggering 16 million tons of wood, much of it old-growth trees cut in Estonia and other places in Eastern Europe with weak environmental regulations and enforcement. The environmentalists concluded: "From an emissions standpoint, the UK would be better off burning coal and leaving those trees standing as long as possible." So much for that idea.

That is one of many reasons I personally find it less than credible that we can suddenly give up on the fossil fuels sector. As long as the demand is there, and it is, barring a collapse-type of economic calamity, starving the sector of capital will just increase prices and/or move investments to other, ecologically worse, sectors. Yes, we can put a price on carbon, as the Singapore government has done, one of 46 countries worldwide to impose a carbon tax, although the only one so far in Southeast Asia, where most fossil fuels are heavily state-subsidized. But will an additional artificial emission price put a dent in demand? Or will it just be another tax that producers and consumers will learn to live with and absorb? That remains to be seen, but I suspect the latter.

And as we saw earlier, when I quoted Jason Hickel of *Less is More* fame, even if we were to completely switch to "renewable" power sources (which in themselves are huge industrialized machinery made using fossil energy and out of non-renewable materials), this will not stop our emissions of CO_2 and other airborne pollutants, if that is your main concern; there are plenty of other sources for that, such as agriculture, forestry and construction. However, in my view, all that shouldn't stop the concerned investor from considering sustainability and ethics in her decisions – there are lots of moving parts in this matter.

THE BAD AND THE UGLY

Regarding ethics, this is an area where investors do appear to have had an impact in reality. In both *Sustainable Investing* and *Your Essential Guide to Sustainable Investing*, the authors point out some of the problems with sustainability and ESG investing, such as the vague definitions in the space and the crowding of capital – the ESG "investment bubble" if you will – but they conclude, and I tend to agree, that much of the recent focus on ESG has been for the better. Not so much on the E side, environmental, but rather on the S (social) and G (governance) aspects of operations, where companies today seem to be better governed and managed than they used to be, with more inclusive HR policies and better control of corrupt practices. A report on Bloomberg concluded: "When integrating ESG into investment strategies, corporate governance is often the starting point, largely because investors understand that governance is the primary non-financial factor that affects financial performance. A 2019 study by the Diligent Institute found that the top fifth of performers on corporate governance in the S&P 500 index outperformed the bottom fifth by 15% over a two-year period. It also found that 'companies with corporate crises fueled by governance deficits underperformed their sectors by 35%, on average, a year after the incident'." [55]

Both investors and consumers can successfully punish companies that misbehave. We will look at the consumer's role in the next chapter, but let me just highlight that for the concerned investor there is plenty to worry about. Virtually all sectors and industries within sectors in our economy have governance and ethical issues; there is lots that needs to be fixed.

I have been to several sustainability seminars where representatives from Swedish-based IKEA (not listed on any exchange) sang the praises of the company's ESG record: All wood is either recycled or FSC-certified, IKEA supports the circular economy, etc ... all the usual you would expect from a sustainability officer worth her salt. Yet, the first claim might be contradicted by reports such as this: "Ikea's Race for the Last of Europe's Old-Growth Forest: The furniture giant is hungry for Romania's famed trees. Little stands in its way." [56] And regarding the second claim, here is a story from real experience. When our son recently finished school, my wife and I wanted to redo his boy's room and sell off the IKEA furniture he had before: an elevated bed with a desktop arrangement underneath. I couldn't find a buyer anywhere on the internet and decided to give it back for free to IKEA. It was basically as good as new, but I was told that IKEA doesn't take stuff back, and I guarantee you that I *really* tried to penetrate to the top management of the company, to no avail. I had to pay the IKEA guys S$80 to come and dismantle the furniture and drive it out for incineration. There goes the circular economy.

Like I said, if you look closely you can find sustainability and ESG issues in all industries, take your pick. Retail, such as Amazon and Walmart? Both have big problems with worker's rights; Walmart is on the Norwegian Oil Fund's exclusion list. Consumer products, like Apple, the biggest company in the world? Here is a report from AFP: "The Paris prosecutor has opened a judicial inquiry into planned obsolescence of Apple products ... [and] deceptive marketing practices".[57] Finance? Heard of the HSBC billion-dollar money laundering scandals?[58] Standard Chartered had 62 bribery and corruption reports in 2021 alone.[59] Groceries? I mentioned Nestlé above in the food business but there are many others out there, companies using excessive amounts of artificial colouring, nitrates and unhealthy and addictive corn syrup in their products, for instance. Transport? Heard of the Volkswagen "Dieselgate" scandals? I am sure you have, so I will not get into this in detail; it turns out that VW was not alone in this type of criminal fraud anyway, blatantly cheating on pollution emission numbers.

Even supposedly "nice" industries like healthcare have issues – we will look at their record of unnecessary and overpriced treatments in the next chapter. Or take agriculture: the mission is to grow healthy and sustainable food for all mankind, right? No, the mission is to make money, sometimes any way they can. Just one case story here will do. Monsanto has long been known for their GMO products and their controversial "terminator" seeds that force farmers to buy new seeds every year; they are not allowed to keep a few from each harvest and replant them. But that is not all: Monsanto also pushes herbicides, i.e. weed-killers, on their customers. In 2018, a judge in California ruled that a groundsman, Dewayne Johnson, contracted cancer from working with a Monsanto weed-killer, RangerPro.[60] The jurors in the case found that Monsanto acted with "malice" and that the weed-killer contributed "substantially" to Mr Johnson's terminal illness. The jury in the eight-week-long trial said the company should have warned users about the dangers of its Roundup and RangerPro products, and ordered Monsanto to pay $40 million in costs and fines and $250 million in punitive damages to Mr Johnson, a total payout of $290 million. Mr Johnson is among more than 5,000 similar plaintiffs across the US awaiting trial. Bayer AG of Germany had just bought Monsanto for $66 billion in June that year, and on the first trading day after the verdict, Bayer's share price dropped 10.4%. Frontier justice, financial ESG style.

THERE IS TOO MUCH MONEY

Before we leave the financial realm, let me highlight one aspect of sustainable investing that is poorly understood. We have too much money in the economy. The enormous expansion of our money supply and super-low interest rates have amounted to "printing money" and this has been going on for decades now. The process started after the 1973 Oil Crisis but accelerated during the Reagan years (1981–89) and never really stopped. After the Great Recession, starting in 2007, the money-printing went into overdrive; it was called QE then, Quantitative Easing, and the deficits kept piling up. During the Covid-19 pandemic, the printing presses were running hot again. For mainstream economists this is no problem; the mantra from the Reagan years was repeated by Vice-President Dick Cheney: "Reagan proved deficits don't matter."[61] It was immaterial who was in charge of the Western world – Republicans or Democrats in the US, Conservatives, Liberals or Social Democrats in Europe – more fiat currency was always the answer to financial trouble. No one seemed to have a problem with this.

When I was young in the 1950s and 1960s, the richest man in the world over a number of years was American oil man Paul Getty; his net worth in 1966 was estimated at $1.2 billion. A billion plus? Today any kid with a clever computer algorithm can become a billionaire. The last time Forbes counted them, there were 2,640 billionaires in the world, with a total capital of $12.2 trillion; six of those were in the triple-digit billionaire category. So what we have now, some 50 years after Getty's long reign, is a lot fewer resources in the world, and a lot more money, most of it simply just debt.

But there *is* a problem with this, many problems in fact. Excess liquidity in the economy can keep the wheels turning, but you cannot eat banknotes or numbers on a computer; the money has to be converted into something tangible to be of any use. That is where environmental limits come in. The money ends up generating uneconomic growth; it inflates asset prices such as stocks, commodities and housing, and thereby also increases social inequality, benefiting mainly those who had assets and were rich already. A house that initially cost X dollars goes up to 10X dollars over a number of years; so the person living there might feel richer, but she is not really better off; the house hasn't changed, has it? In fact, it should have dropped in price over the years. When my grandfather was young, some 100 years ago, houses in Europe were seen as a liability – with all the maintenance required, eventually the place would have to be torn down. That generation saw *land* as a valuable asset, but not buildings. When Getty was around, an ounce of gold was $35 (today, last time I checked, it is $1,970); a barrel of crude oil – the substance that made Getty so rich – was $3.10 a barrel in 1966, pretty much unchanged for decades; today it is $74, although fluctuating wildly. You can print dollar bills, but you cannot print gold and oil and food and other stuff.

And that leads us to the issue of return on investments. Few seem to consider this, but David Ko and Richard Busellato do. In their book, *The Unsustainable Truth: How Investing for the Future is Destroying the Planet and What to do About it* (2021), they establish that surveys and reports in 2020 estimated "global investment assets" to be worth $101.7 trillion. And "investors from half of the 32 countries surveyed are expecting a return of over 10.93", that is percent per annum. So the authors do the math: "Applying the 10.93% return expected to the $101.7 trillion of assets means we are expecting our savings to grow by more than $11 trillion a year. This is about the size of the combined GDP of Germany, the UK, France and Italy". There is no way the Earth can produce that kind of financial return year after year; the real economy is simply not growing fast enough to provide the return we are expecting.

"When we grow by more than 1% per annum," Ko and Busellato write, "we are using resources faster than the capacity our planet currently has to replenish them ... When we are saying we are moving to sustainable growth, we are proposing that we can increase the capacity of what our planet can provide. It does not come about simply because we are putting vast amounts of money into it."

The authors provide case stories for how the desperate search for yield is damaging local economies and the environment. They mention wine-growing, which is supposed to be an enduring, slow-moving process, traditionally operated by family-owned small farms. But as pension funds start buying up vineyards, this is now being accelerated and force-fed with unsuitable artificial irrigation techniques which produce tasteless grapes and damage the water supply in the often semi-arid wine-growing regions. All in the name of quick profits and higher returns on excess capital. Another example is the property market, where hot money managed by large global investment firms like Blackrock (with some $10 trillion in assets, and always looking for yield) are buying up rental units, bidding up the property in cities all over the world, to the point where ordinary people can hardly afford to live. "Portugal is currently grappling with a severe housing crisis, triggered by an increase in foreign investment in property and a lack of affordable new homes," the BBC announced in May 2023, but this is true for many countries, not just Portugal.[62]

The global cryptocurrency market is worth $1.14 trillion, with about half of that in Bitcoin.[63] The gold market is worth $13.5 trillion.[64] Stocks on the NYSE are worth $25.2 trillion, those on

Nasdaq another $19 trillion.[65] The P/E ratio on the S&P 500 blue-chip stocks is currently 29, about 43% above the historical average, even with war in Europe and a debt crisis looming indicating a bubble.[66] The US national debt is $31 trillion (see Chapter 2). So we are printing trillions and trillions of Dollars and Euros and Pounds and Yen, and we are expecting all of them to make a return – of 10.93% per annum? This way, our economy is looking more and more like one giant Ponzi scheme.

Few in the financial industry seem to worry about this, but Ko and Busellato do, so I will give them the last word on sustainability in this chapter: "Sustainability has taken on the shape of a universal cause; even cluster munition manufacturers have corporate social responsibility action plans that promote it as they advertise the horrible killing power of their products. We cannot rely on businesses and governments to make the world into what we need. Lots of small actions on our part have made the world into what it is, and it will be the small actions on our part that will determine what the world will be." We will look at some of the "small actions" you can take in the next chapter.

6

Your Lifestyle: Can It Be Sustained?

BUT WHAT IF GROWTH DOESN'T WORK?

We have seen that in Singapore economic growth is "non-nego-tiable". In fact, it is in all countries that I know of, in all commercial companies operating and in all the central banks around the world regulating them. Our system is built on economic growth and I would estimate that about 99% of the world's population support this. How do I arrive at this number? In 2019, the *Straits Times* reported: "Big turnout at Hong Lim Park for first Singapore Climate Rally."[67] The organizers estimated that 2,000 people turned up "as they called on the Singapore Government and firms here to do more to reduce planet-warming greenhouse gas emissions". I suppose those attendants might be willing to sacrifice a bit of economic growth for less atmospheric pollution damaging the climate and our collective future. As it happened, that weekend was also the Singapore Grand Prix Formula 1 race.

Just across from Hong Lim Park, the race was a complete sell-out. Unlike the climate rally, those visitors actually had to pay, anywhere from S$98 for a single-day ticket to as much as S$268 for all three days of the event. Some 300,000 fans attended the race, the highest attendance in the 13-year history of the Singapore F1 stage.[68] If I can presume those people were not so concerned about carbon emissions or global warming or the detrimental effects of economic growth, then you would have a 2,000/300,000 ratio of the public voting with their feet, exhibiting these opposing values. That is about 0.66%, but let me be generous and round up and conclude: 1% of people care seriously about the environment.

It doesn't really matter how incredibly rich we have become; seen by historical standards, we always want more. The IMF expects 3.1–3.4% global economic growth going forward, which it considers "subpar" economic growth.[69] Well, 3.25% p.a. average economic growth will double the world economy in 22 years: double the number of cars, double the number of houses, double the number of smartphones, double the amount of food and of everything else. Of course that is not possible; so we really just pretend we are growing, by inflating the numbers and imagining that we are better off that way. Economic growth has become like pushing on a string.

I get it. If you really want to be sustainable and climate-friendly and all that, you should live like people do in Eritrea, East Timor and North Korea – these countries have some of the smallest ecological footprints of all. Burundi is not far behind, living well within their sustainability means; but would you like to live there? The GDP per capita in Burundi is currently estimated at $308,[70] and it has been declining steadily since 1991.[71] The overall global GDP per capita is currently $13,920, but 123 countries, more than half, have GDP below the global average. Except, I don't see a lot of people lining up to get into North Korea or Burundi, the way they do at the Mexico/Texas border. I am sure a lot of people could not even find Burundi on a map, yet on paper it is a role model for ecological sustainability, while also the poorest country in the world. Surely this doesn't make sense.

NET-ZERO OIL?

So we can agree that most people don't want to live in Burundi or in North Korea. They want to go on enjoying the good life, consuming and growing, but in a sustainable way. Is that possible? In *This Changes Everything* (2015), Naomi Klein observes that our recent incredible economic growth has been undeniably linked to fossil fuel consumption and carbon emissions. But if prosperity = emissions, then Klein concludes that less emissions = less prosperity; this is fairly logical, right? Enter the sustainability mantra: We can keep growing if we do it in a sustainable manner.

There is just one problem with that, as we have seen before: real decoupling (between physical resource use and prosperity) is not happening. The concept of "net zero" too often involves sleight-of-hand calculations that don't hold up under scrutiny. Part of net-zero is that the polluter keeps polluting, but then supports "green" schemes elsewhere as an "offset" project. First of all, there are plenty of horror stories about failed REDD (Reducing Emissions from Deforestation and Forest Degradation) projects, and I mention a few of them in my last book, *The Ethical Investor's*

Handbook. But secondly, again this is a problem of scale. Ko and Busellato, who wrote *The Unsustainable Truth*, which I refer to in the previous chapter, are not ecologists, they are numbers guys; so they point out that there simply aren't enough green projects in the world to ever offset a fraction of the pollution that needs to be "neutralized". What is happening is that multiple companies buy into the same small feeble projects which simply cannot move the needle sufficiently.

But that is OK, because we will just move the targets so far out into the future that it buys us time to go on with business as usual for a little while longer. We will be carbon-neutral by 2030, and if that doesn't work, by 2050.

Occidental Petroleum CEO Vicki Hollub has been touring the media circuit for some time now explaining how Oxy's oil production will be net-zero soon, and their chemical business as well, for good measure. One report on Bloomberg says: "Rather than reducing oil and gas production, Oxy wants to make net-zero oil by investing heavily in carbon-capture technology."[72] Wow, net-zero oil, did I hear that right? You can still find that interview online – see if you can make head or tail of it.[73] Hollub explains that by collecting generous (deficit-financed) government subsidies, selling carbon credits and by capturing CO_2 from the air and injecting it into the underground formation, the whole company will go carbon-neutral and still remain highly profitable. She also expects to be able to produce oil and gas from Oxy's leases in the Permian Basin (western Texas and New Mexico) for "the next 40–50 years". That last bit I believe; the other statements not so much.

YOUR LIFESTYLE: CAN IT BE SUSTAINED?

There is zero-carbon bunker fuel for shipping. Does that sound bonkers? I am not kidding; here is one report from the Port of Long Beach, California: "The Maritime and Port Authority of Singapore (MPA), Port of Long Beach, Port of Los Angeles, and C40 Cities have begun discussions to establish a green and digital shipping corridor between Singapore and the San Pedro Bay port complex. The corridor will focus on low- and zero-carbon ship fuels, as well as digital tools to support deployment of low- and zero-carbon ships."[74] Zero-carbon ships? Is that a rowing boat? Even in a rowing boat, the person doing the rowing will emit some CO_2.

The aviation industry is into this as well, desperately trying to go about business as usual; no, not business as usual, *expanding* the business, while paying homage to the greenies. The weapon of choice here is SAF, Sustainable Aviation Fuel. All the big guns are in on this: ExxonMobil, BP, Honeywell as well as government aviation and transport authorities everywhere. Always on the lookout for another FDI opportunity, Singapore's Economic Development Board announced in 2022: "Singapore would have the world's largest sustainable aviation fuel (SAF) production capacity when Finnish producer Neste's Tuas facility is completed in the first quarter of 2023. Neste can produce as much as 1 million metric tonnes of fuel a year when the €1.5b refinery in Tuas is completed in 2023. SAF is a fuel produced from renewable raw materials, such as used cooking oil, or animal fat from food industry waste. It meets all quality and performance requirements of conventional fossil fuels but costs 3 to 5 times more."[75]

Right, 1 million tonnes of fuel seems like a lot, but in 2022, global commercial aviation consumption of jet fuel was estimated at roughly 200 million tonnes (converted from 60 billion gallons).[76] This is *not* counting private and military consumption, which is substantial. And to put this further into perspective, on the website from Airbus you find this statement: "Since 2011, SAF has powered more than 450,000 commercial flights around the world. However, global SAF production represents 0.03% of fuel use (based on pre-pandemic numbers) and in 2021, was less than 1% of operated flights."[77] One wonders, how much used cooking oil and dead animals are there out there, so that the industry can fulfil this pledge: "In October 2022, member states of the International Civil Aviation Organization (ICAO) agreed to a long-term aspirational goal (LTAG) of net-zero carbon dioxide (CO_2) emissions from aviation by 2050."[78] There it is again: push out the so-called LTAG far enough for few of us to be around by the time the day of reckoning arrives.

Maybe it's just me, but personally I would take the many lofty promises from industry with a grain of salt. I also don't find growing more oil palm to burn or grinding more animals into fuel particularly ethically acceptable, economical, "green" or even sustainable. The BBC reported that it would take fat from 8,800 dead pigs to power a flight from Paris to New York.[79] That's a lot of pigs; maybe we should start to consider using fat from people instead – but then we would be moving into *Soylent Green* territory, the dystopian movie I mentioned in Chapter 1.

And actually, it's not just me. In 2022 you could read, also on BBC: "Environmental groups are suing Dutch airline KLM, alleging that adverts promoting the company's sustainability initiative are misleading. They argue that KLM adverts and their carbon-offsetting scheme create the false impression that its flights won't make climate change worse ... 'Flight emissions cannot be "compensated" if customers just pay extra to plant trees or give money towards the cost of false solutions like what the industry calls "sustainable aviation fuels" ... Unchecked flying is one of the fastest ways to heat up the planet. Customers need to be informed and protected from claims that suggest it is not.'"[80] Maybe one day consumer groups will examine the recent similar claims from the shipping industry and check to see if they hold up in court.

WE MIGHT BE IN THE ANTHROPOCENE

I am not saying that we shouldn't try to make aviation and other transport and travel more efficient and less wasteful and polluting, of course we should. We should also try to create jobs for all the sustainability graduates and environmental engineers pouring out from our universities, they need stuff to fiddle with. I am just with Alan Jackson when he says: "But here in the *real* world, it's not that easy at all."[81] So I am only urging everyone to keep an eye on the big picture.

Ian Angus does that, he looks at the big picture. I don't agree with everything that Angus promotes in his 2016 book, *Facing the Anthropocene*, but I find his description of the era we are in informative and useful. As you might know, geologists use what is called the geological time scale to structure the Earth's 4.5-billion-year history into eons, eras, periods, epochs and ages. Today we are in the Holocene epoch, which began some 11,700 years ago, with the end of the last ice age. Prior to that we were in the Pleistocene epoch, characterized by regular warming and cooling periods associated with expanding and contracting ice sheets around the poles and high mountain ranges. Now, the eggheads in the International Commission on Stratigraphy, the commission that has the responsibility for determining and describing the geological time scale, are considering whether we have entered a new epoch, the Anthropocene.

This is a big deal. The experts generally agree that things have changed, that we are now in a time where human activities are affecting the nature of the planet. They point out that:

1. Since crude oil was discovered as a fuel around 1850, atmospheric concentrations of CO_2 have exceeded historic Holocene levels and have accelerated 100 times faster than was "normal" before then; the same for methane and other greenhouse gases as well.

2. While the Earth should really be cooling now, due to changes in the tilt of its axis and the orbital cycle around the sun, global air and water temperatures are not coming down. By some estimates, a new ice age should be on its way 1,500 years from now, except it doesn't seem to go that way; temperatures have increased by some 0.9°C since 1900 instead, and the increases are accelerating. Anthropogenic global warming seems to be overwhelming the natural cooling cycle.

3. Sea levels started rising around 1905 and are now at their highest in 115,000 years – and the rise is accelerating.

YOUR LIFESTYLE: CAN IT BE SUSTAINED?

4. Biodiversity is declining. We are losing species at a rate of 1,000 times normally expected; we could lose 75% of all species within the next few hundred years, which would be the sixth major extinction event in the history of the Earth and the largest since the dinosaurs disappeared some 65 million years ago.

If all this is indeed "man-made", that would really put us in a new epoch, the Anthropocene, i.e. the period where man shaped the structure of the natural environment and essentially altered the Earth. What the scientists cannot agree on is when this transition began, so although many people are using this term, it cannot be officially confirmed yet. Some say that the new epoch started already shortly after the last ice cover retreated, when humans began to grow the land and build villages and towns, so that Holocene should really just be renamed. Others, and that is maybe the majority, think that the Anthropocene started as recently as the mid-1900s, with the first nuclear bomb test and the economic growth after World War II. As we saw, around 1950 is the starting point of the Great Acceleration, and as such it was this expansion that definitively caused anthropogenic changes which altered the geology, geography and biology of the Earth, to the point of no return.

I have heard that some 95% of Earth scientists believe that climate change is man-made. I am no climatologist, but I find it intuitively logical that when more than half of the Earth's surface is altered by man, this will have consequences. The Geological Society of America says: "The expansion of infrastructure and agriculture necessitated by this population growth has quickened the pace of land transformation and degradation. We estimate that humans have modified >50% of Earth's land surface. The current rate of land transformation, particularly of agricultural land, is unsustainable. We need a lively public discussion of the problems resulting from population pressures and the resulting land degradation."[82] Our atmosphere is paper-thin; when you cruise at 30,000 feet in a commercial jet you can see the edge of our oxygen layer; it is obvious to me that our pollutants must be changing the composition of it.

So like everyone else I read the alarming reports about climate change and global warming. But unlike many, I am just not too worried about it. I try to examine myself for fear, but sorry, I cannot find any. I think we will be alright. Did you know that the Earth was once covered in ice? Yes, 650–700 million years ago, so the hypothesis has it, the ice caps went from the poles all the way to the Equator. That must have been a pretty tough time to live in, yet life survived. You can Google "snowball Earth" for the details. According to the theory, volcanic eruptions broke through the ice, increased the atmospheric CO_2 level and reanimated life on Earth. Then a little while later, 90 million years ago, during the Late Cretaceous Period, what do you know: there was no ice on Earth at all! The North Pole was covered in lush forest, and dinosaurs roamed around Antarctica.[83] CO_2 levels were then around 1,000 ppm; if we keep going like we are now, we will get back to that point eventually.[84] Back then, sea levels were 170 metres higher than today; the highest point in Singapore is 164 metres above sea level; and now we worry about a 1 metre rise?

I realize that by geological time standards, changes to our environment are happening at a much higher speed than usual. That is because we are contributing to the changes. But so what? We just have to adapt quickly as well. Since we are part of the problem, we must also be part of the solution. And if we cannot find a solution, which we apparently cannot, then we just have to make the best of the circumstances.

THE SUSTAINABLE CONSUMER

Individually, we cannot control the climate, but we can change our response to events and adjust our lifestyle and our habits. It would be easier for all of us if we weren't so many people and if each of us used slightly less resources. But that can be arranged. In the new economy and the new environment, there will be winners and there will be some who don't win quite as much. I was poor once, so I realize that you don't really need that much stuff around you. There are other things in life that can make you happy, apart from objects. I mentioned Chris Martenson of peakprosperity.com earlier; Richard Heinberg with the Post Carbon Institute think-tank has similar ideas – he wrote *Peak Everything: Waking Up to the Century of Declines* (2010) as well as *The End of Growth: Adapting to Our New Economic Reality* (2011). Just in case Martenson, Heinberg and other strategists like that are right, in case we are heading deep into the Century of Declines, we should position ourselves accordingly. I find it very unlikely that my Gen Y and Z kids will see the same explosive expansion in wealth most Baby Boomers did. But then, the young people today don't really need such an escalation: most grew up with everything they needed given to them. I think we are moving from the Great Acceleration into the Great Stagnation, and we simply have to accept that.

This transition, from acceleration to stagnation, will be a lot smoother and more painless if we each of us adjust our lifestyle accordingly. Ko and Busellato (2021), whom I mentioned before, had their careers in the financial industry, and in their book they object to the prevailing attitude there: Leave nothing on the table for others; winner takes it all. They ask somewhat innocently: What is wrong with leaving a bit on the table for others?

As consumers we could ask the same thing: What is wrong with giving our suppliers a fair deal? Sometimes we have to be prepared to pay a little bit more for "fair trade" products where producers, growers and suppliers are treated reasonably and honestly. Agricultural products, handicrafts and even gold bullion and jewellery come in fair trade versions.

In general, the best thing you can really do for sustainability is: spend less. It is that simple! My four kids grew up with what they needed, but I should add that there was one little thing I did different from most parents: I never gave them presents. No boxes nicely wrapped under the Christmas tree, nothing for birthdays. The rest of their family gave them plenty of made-in-China toys and junk, but they got none of that from me. I didn't want to confuse material gifts with love. So I did things with my kids instead, I gave them my time. I took them out playing and travelling, to basketball and football and Taekwondo and badminton games, running and swimming and cycling. I took them to school and picked them up, day after day, year after year; after school we did chores and mowed the lawn and read books and watched TV together; my kids were never allowed to watch TV on their own. I had much more fun that way, and I hope they did too.

I told you, I am in no position to point fingers at others. I have contributed, probably more than most, to resource depletion, pollution and man-made global warming – let's assume for a moment that there really is such a thing. But now and then it does strike me as odd, that some of those who demand the government to do more to fix environmental problems are also sometimes those who queue up for the latest iPhone, while the old one goes in the trash. Every day shoppers scrutinize the internet for the latest 2-for-1 bargains of things they don't need; then complain about price inflation and not enough in pay.

It is demand that is driving our unsustainable lifestyle. Not big business and not the governments – they just respond to the demands of consumers and voters, respectively. Commercial companies can try to stimulate sales with adverts and manipulation, but they cannot force people to buy. Politicians can campaign all they want, but at the end of the day it is still the people who have the final say. As Joseph de Maistre said: "Every country has the government it deserves."[85] And you could say the same thing about consumers: Every purchaser has the supplier he/she deserves.

Let us consider the plastic menace. We don't really need plastic; I know this because when I was a child there wasn't any and we managed alright! On top of that, the evidence is overwhelming that plastic is one of the nastiest and most harmful substances ever invented by man. We are regularly bombarded with horror stories about plastics filling the rivers and the oceans, eaten by birds and fishes and eventually by ourselves; less than 10% is recycled, which is fine because the logistics, processes and resource use involved in recycling makes it counterproductive.

So we should be using less plastic, right? Of course, but are we? Not according to this report on CNN: "The world generated 139 million metric tons of single-use plastic waste in 2021, which was 6 million metric tons more than in 2019 ... driven by demand for flexible packaging like films and sachets. In recent years, governments around the world have announced policies to reduce the volume of single-use plastic, banning products like single-use straws, disposable cutlery, food containers, cotton swabs, bags and balloons. But the report found that recycling isn't scaling up fast enough to deal with the amount of plastic being produced, meaning that used products are far more likely to be dumped in landfills, on beaches and in rivers and oceans than to make it into recycling plants."[86]

And here is a chart to confirm the CNN report:

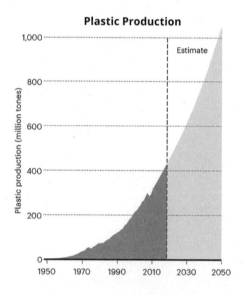

So it appears that plastic production/consumption is expected to double from now and until the magic year of 2050, when we allegedly will finally be completely carbon-neutral and sustainable. There are retail shops here in Singapore where you bring your own reusable containers for items such as food and soaps, to reduce the packaging, but I have never been inside one of them. In the real world, we all flock to the conventional supermarkets for the convenience and low prices.

One thing about this country, Singapore, is that at least we don't chuck our plastic into the nearest river, like people in so many other countries in Asia do. We don't even dump it in a landfill; we don't have the space. So we incinerate the plastic, and being made out of oil it burns just fine in waste-to-energy plants. The ashes are carefully deposited on a designated offshore island from where they cannot seep into the environment. I am aware that you could argue that burning plastic is toxic, I am sure it is. But in a less-than-perfect world, I personally find that outcome to be the least-evil solution to the plastic menace and I wish they would put up more such incinerators in Indonesia, a country where I worked for many years and will always love, but which is being completely beleaguered by the plastic plague.

Back in the supermarket, products on the shelves labelled "sustainable" or "ethical" are OK for consumers; in fact, for most it seems that they are preferable; only not so much if they cost extra. In a report on the *eco-business* website, the journalist writes: "Global demand for more environmentally-friendly and ethically-made products should influence more companies to drive sustainability initiatives and make their claims more public. However, as climate change and other environmental issues such as waste and plastic pollution become a growing concern for Asian consumers, sustainable products are now more popular in the region than ever before. Half of consumers in Southeast Asia would pay more for environmentally-friendly products, according to a global survey conducted by Nielsen in 2017. That alone might suggest that sustainable products are taking off in the region. But are Asian consumers putting their money where their mouth is? 'Consumers voice positive opinion for sustainable products but don't back it up at the check-out counter,' said Regan Leggett, executive director of thought leadership and foresight at Nielsen, a global measurement and data analytics company. 'But if the price is competitive for two brands, sustainability could be the deciding factor.'"[87] I rest my case.

BIG-TICKET ITEMS 1: HOUSES

I have mentioned housing before, while making the point that it is in some ways a historical oddity and an abomination that property keeps going up in our new economy, mainly driven by population expansion and debt. But although in many ways an unmerited situation, this is something you have to accept and adjust to. Since property prices over time keep increasing, you really have to own your home if you want to be sustainable. You might rent for a while, when you are young and mobile and your circumstances change frequently, but in the long run you do not want to be caught out on the rental market, vulnerable to the whims of landlords. In May 2023, BBC ran this story about the rental property market in Singapore: "'Doomsday': Singapore renters sound the alarm as prices surge" – the headline says it all.[88] The situation might be similar in New York and London and San Francisco and many other cities with opportunities, where tenants end up spending half their paychecks just to get a small apartment to hole up in.

So secure your own place if you can, within your financial means, and thereby lock in the rent for the future, until you finally pay off that mortgage and only have the property taxes and maintenance to worry about, hopefully long before you retire. In *Be Financially Free*, I cover in more detail the finer points of property investments, including aspects of investing in multiple properties and REITS.

Keep in mind that although the world population is continuously growing, not all cities and countries and areas are expanding; some are contracting. Demographia.com has an interesting list of municipalities around the world with declining populations; many well-known names are down by 20%, 30% or even 40% from their peak a few decades ago.[89] A place like that may not be the best to invest in. While people are generally flocking to the big cities, where the job opportunities are, many rural areas are not so hot. In Japan, there is a term for unwanted houses in rural districts: *akiya*, "empty house", and there are millions of them. One report said: "As Japan's population shrinks and more properties go unclaimed, an emerging segment of buyers, feeling less tethered to overcrowded cities, is seeking out rural architecture in need of some love. The most recent government data, from the 2018 Housing and Land survey, reported about 8.5 million akiya across the country – roughly 14 per cent of the country's housing stock – but observers say there are many more today. The Nomura Research Institute puts the number at more than 11 million, and predicts that akiya could exceed 30 per cent of all houses in Japan by 2033."[90] The empty houses come cheap and often have some land around them, but restoring them can be a money pit, and their future value is uncertain as well, so *caveat emptor*, buyer beware!

The leasehold of the land that your dream home is sitting on is also a factor you should consider, before signing on the dotted line of that sales contract. In a place like Singapore, the government owns much of the land and doesn't sell it. Many of the private apartment blocks, and all of the public housing, sit on leasehold land, usually 99 years. While that might seem like a long time off if you buy a new place, the day of reckoning will come sooner or later. Since leasehold places naturally sell at lower prices than freehold houses and condos, you might be financially better off getting one of those – provided you know how to make the money you save grow. That way you, or your descendants, will have a nest-egg to find a new home once the value of your place goes to zero.

BIG-TICKET ITEMS 2:
CARS

Apart from your house, your car will probably be the most expensive item you buy. I bought my first car, an Opel station wagon (where I could sleep in the back during road trips) for NOK8,000 ($730) when I was 22 years old. No, it wasn't new, but it held together until I could trade it in for another pre-loved vehicle a few years later, a Ford Capri manual 2.0L, which set me back DKK16,000 ($2,300). I worked for three months in a manual job and then I could buy a car like that. If a young man where I live today should buy a European few-years-old 2.0L coupe, it would cost him about S$90,000 (some US$70,000); even with a good job he would probably have to work more than a year to make that kind of money. So, I get it, we are much richer today than we were in the 1970s; it is just that all that monetary wealth is difficult to convert into real stuff, like houses and cars. Welcome to the economics of a "full world", as Herman Daly says.

In Singapore, cars are now rationed. To get a so-called Certificate of Entitlement (COE), you have to put in a bid. The price for this COE fluctuates wildly with market conditions, supply and demand, but at last week's bidding (17 May 2023) it landed at S$92,000 for a small car (below 1.6L) and S$113,034 for a big-engine model. So you have to pay about $70,000 just to go shopping for a small car, then comes the car itself plus an Additional Registration Fee tax that varies between 100% and 320% of the Open Market Value. Sorry, car lovers, the Singapore roads are full up and vehicle prices reflect that. In other countries, cars might be less heavily taxed, but the motorists still pay a price for the "full world" syndrome in the form of perpetual massive traffic jams! A friend of mine who moved to San Diego a few years back told me that he no longer goes birdwatching in the hills these days: the drive into habitat near the city that should take 20 minutes takes more than two hours now, crawling through a sea of other vehicles on the freeways. After the walk it is another two hours back. While cars might be cheaper in other big cities (other than Singapore), there are usually different constraints, such as exorbitant parking fees or no parking places at all in the city centre, to discourage car ownership and use.

Ah, but now we will just convert all the combustion engine cars to electric vehicles (EVs) and then we will be sustainable, right?

I admit it: I got caught up in the craze when mass-produced hybrid cars were introduced in Singapore. In 2006, when the second-generation Toyota Prius was launched here, my wife and I went out and bought one of those. We were featured in a magazine as the poster-family for Prius owners, and I was interviewed by the daily paper and quoted on the front page singing the praises of hybrid engine technology. I described how cool it was that the vehicle stored energy generated by deceleration and shut down at the lights.

Today I am not so sure. My wife and I had the Prius for 15 years and put some 200,000 km on the clock; it was an impressive piece of engineering. But it also gave us a lot of problems: it was heavy and technically complex and costly. The hybrid system malfunctioned multiple times. After eight years we had to replace the huge lithium battery at the cost of some S$4,000. So when the second COE expired in 2021, we didn't want another hybrid; it simply wasn't as "green" as it was made out to be. For the kind of city driving we do, the hybrid was massively overpowered; you could make do with the 1.5L petrol engine on its own, you didn't really need the additional electric motor at all, plus all the extra batteries, wiring and instrumentation; it was simply a waste of natural resources, labour and financial capital. We ended up buying a Honda Fit for a lot less money, which only has a 1.3L engine that performs excellently, and the consumption is 18km/L. The Prius gave us 22km/L, but that difference is insignificant compared to all the other environmental and economic and man-hour costs involved in this unnecessarily complex machine. The Prius had a curb weight of 1,295 kg; the Honda Fit is 1,010 kg; the extra 285 kg of stuff that the Prius hauls around with it everywhere it goes is just excess fat.

When I shared this news on Facebook, my cousin Jens in Denmark asked me why we didn't get a full Electric Vehicle (EV), my wife and I being such "green" people and all. He bragged that he had just bought a brand-new Volkswagen (full electric) ID.4. I reminded Jens about the Dieselgate criminality that VW was involved in: they promoted dirty diesel cars as "green" and I suspected that now they were trying the same trick with EVs. The monstrous ID.4 SUV has a curb weight of 2,149 kg; the energy budget for transporting Jens and his wife around town in something like that simply doesn't make sense. Yes, when my cousin charges his enormous SUV, about half of the power in his local grid comes from "renewable" energy sources like wind turbines and solar panels. However, you could argue that with the limited lifespan of these "green" machines, made mainly from fossil fuels, this process might not be as sustainable as it appears. Without generous government support, I doubt that my cousin – or many other customers for that matter – could afford an EV. There is a reason why EVs are expensive: the material, labour and capital input is simply excessive. So the government takes funds from the productive sectors of the economy and transfers them into the "electric transformation". That might be good for keeping the big industrial wheels turning for a little while longer, spurring on temporary economic growth, but not so good for the overall economic sustainability or for the environment.

Take this article on the rainforest-rescue.org website: "While the emissions of conventional cars are terrible for the environment and human health, electric vehicles are anything but clean – their production requires an enormous input of energy and raw materials. About 1,800 kilograms of metals and other materials are used in a mid-range electric car such as the Chevrolet Bolt, which is marketed in Europe as the Vauxhall/Opel Ampera-e. The European automotive industry imports almost 100% of these materials – and a significant share of them come from mines in tropical countries and rainforest areas. Lithium-ion batteries, the heart of electric vehicles, are no exception here. The Chevrolet Volt battery pack, for example, weighs 440 kg. Besides lithium, manganese and graphite, they contain about 10 kg of cobalt and 30 kg of nickel. In the case of nickel mining, Indonesia and the Philippines are at the forefront of global production. Two-thirds of the world's cobalt comes from the Democratic Republic of Congo. Cobalt, copper and nickel are mined along an 800-kilometer belt in the rainforest in the south of the country – under catastrophic working conditions, at starvation wages, and by tens of thousands of child laborers. The mines of international corporations are thus eating into the rainforests to satisfy the resource hunger of the manufacturers of 'clean' electric vehicles. Simply clogging the roads with millions of EVs is not the answer to our present problems."[91]

At my condo, we have exactly 144 parking lots in the basement car park. At night the car park is full. I walk around and I see two or three other small cars like ours; there are two small hybrids as well. The rest are massively overpowered monster machines: Lexus, Volvo, BMW, Mercedes, with huge engines, each car can hardly fit into the allocated lot. My neighbours especially love SUVs with gigantic, heavy bodies and oversized wheels, built to plough through a foot and a half of snow. We rarely get that much snow in Singapore. The trend is confirmed by the IEA: Global SUV sales increased from 16.5% of overall sales in 2010 to 45.9% in 2021, and "SUVs rank among the top causes of energy-related carbon dioxide emissions growth over the last decade".[92] I believe in democracy and freedom of choice; I don't think it is the government's job to tell us what to do or what not to do. I just look at my friends and their preference of transport and I have to accept that environmental conservation is not really foremost on their minds; that is all there is to it. Forcing them into buying electric monstrosities instead of combustion engine monstrosities is not going to change that.

IN SICKNESS AND IN HEALTH

There was a cartoon I saw once that has stuck with me. One guy says to another: "What do you think about the world situation?" And his friend answers: "Nothing – I've got something in my eye." If you are sick, nothing else really matters; you cannot be sustainable if you are not physically well.

I am lucky to live in Singapore where we spend only 4.5% of GDP on healthcare (*The Economist*, 2021). In my native Denmark it is 10.1%, and in the US it is an astronomical 16.9%. Yet, by all conventional health measures, such as life expectancy and infant mortality rate, Singapore is above Denmark and even more above the US. It seems that the amount you spend on healthcare is inversely proportional to the outcome.

This is true for nations, but I suspect it is true for individuals as well. I am no health expert, but I have observed over the years that those people who fuss over their health and spend a lot of money on tests and treatments are also often the ones with the worst outcome. I sincerely believe that doctors in general are fine people who really want the best for their patients. All the doctors

I have ever met, privately as well as during consultations, have fallen into that category. Except one senior orthopaedic surgeon who examined my knee after a sports injury many years ago and wanted to operate on it. I objected and walked out of there, and the knee healed itself over time.

But having said that, I will also point out that much of the health industry as a whole is just that: another industry where profits reign supreme. In the investment chapter earlier, I hinted at some of the unethical practices going on, even in healthcare, and there are plenty of case stories to back that up. Here is a story reported in the Danish newspaper *Jyllandsposten* that I read sometimes (my own translation): "Way too many people are being treated with medication, examinations and operation that they don't require. Such goes the evaluation by some 450 researchers from 30 different countries who recently visited Copenhagen to attend the conference on Preventing Overdiagnostication 2018. 'The unnecessary treatments not only cost money, they also make life worse for the patients,' says Dr John Brodersen; he has researched overdiagnostication for 15 years and was one of the promoters of the conference. ... The method of payment that awards larger fees to doctors treating many patients in a short time contributes to the problems of over-treatment. 'If you want to be a successful doctor, you have to treat as many as possible as much as possible and as quickly as possible,' Dr Brodersen adds. 'If you want to be a decent doctor, you should do the opposite and spend more time on fewer patients.'"[93] A profit-based/insurance-financed healthcare system like in the US encourages waste and over-medication, leading to more illness, medicine dependency, more profits for the pharmaceutical industry and more suffering and earlier death for the population in general.

In my view, the Covid-19 episode was one such classic case of healthcare mismanagement. Regarding the pandemic period, we all have a sad story to tell, I suppose; I know I have a few. I was prevented from attending my father's funeral in Norway because of lockdowns and travel restrictions when he died in February 2021. I found that over the top, unreasonable and unfair but there was nothing I could do. And here is another one: I have never been arrested in my life until I came back from Alaska in late September 2021; then I finally had to go to "jail". My offence was travelling abroad during the pandemic. In spite of three negative tests during the trip and on arrival back in Singapore, I and a few others were escorted by people in raincoats and face shields to the JW Marriott, Beach Road, where I was confined to my room for 10 days; the windows wouldn't open and I wasn't allowed out into the hall. A note on the table said that if I left the room for any reason, my PR status in Singapore would be revoked immediately. Every day, three square meals were left outside my room; if I opened the door too quickly during the delivery, the hotel staff would scuttle away hastily to avoid me like the plague.

I couldn't help thinking that the pandemic response was somewhat overplayed. I personally believe that Sweden adopted the right policies by keeping lockdowns and masking and vaccination mandates to the bare minimum. Although I'm not against either face masks or vaccinations or isolations, I think this is better left up to the individual. If you don't want to, don't go out; if you feel better that way, get vaccinated and wear a mask; we don't *all* have to, do we? I am not completely alone in these views. Robert F. Kennedy, who wrote *The Real Anthony Fauci: Bill Gates, Big Pharma, and the Global War on Democracy and Public Health* (2021), seems to think the same way.

It is easy to dismiss Kennedy as a crackpot and a conspiracy theorist, but I believe he has a strong case. He is not a nobody, he is the son of the greatest president the US never had. His father of the same name got assassinated in 1968 shortly before a presidential election that he was destined to win; Nixon won that year instead and the rest is history. We need contrarians like Robert Kennedy Jr to speak up and start a debate: "the system" is not always right. Those of us who remember the Y2K episode will know. That was when "the system" warned us about impending doom as we moved into the year 2000; atomic reactors the world over would implode and planes fall out of the sky because computers allegedly couldn't cope with the change of year and century. That never happened; those countries that ignored the issue and spent nothing on Y2K preparations came out ahead. Of course I took my Covid-19 shots like everyone else and obeyed the rules, out of respect for our elected government. I just don't agree with the way the whole pandemic was handled worldwide.

I am not worried about flu viruses and bugs. There were a lot of bugs going around when I was growing up in the 1950s, as I suppose there are now. But when my big sister got sick, my mother wouldn't isolate me from her. She would put me up in her bunk bed and let us sleep together for a while to make sure I got exposed to the germs as well. She said it was better if I got the common childhood illnesses over with quickly while young. I am so thankful that my mother did that, I am sure it improved my immune system tremendously.

And I do agree with the governments and the mainstream media when they keep warning us that the next pandemic is on its way. Or make that the next crisis certainly; if it is not a pandemic, then it might be a war or a financial or natural disaster. So be a "doomsday prepper": prepare practically, financially and mentally for the Next Big One. But at the same time, appreciate life while it is good and consider joining the FIRE movement.

7

Join the FIRE Movement

FINANCIAL INDEPENDENCE

As we have seen so far, if you are really concerned about our sustainability – financially, environmentally and as a coherent society – the best thing you can do is spend less. By spending less, you conserve precious natural resources so that there will be more for future generations. You also save financial capital, which will enable you to join the FIRE movement so much sooner. That is, the Financial Independence Retire Early interest group. When I wrote *Be Financially Free* in 2016, I didn't even know that such a movement existed, but I know now, sometimes great minds think alike; it turns out that what appeared intuitively right to me from an early age – spend less, retire early and do what you love – also resonates with lots of other people.

"The basic template goes something like this," the BBC reported in 2018. "Proponents live as frugally as possible, saving half their income or more during their 20s or 30s. The aim is to retire in their 30s, or 40s at the latest ... Although these ideas have been around for many years, online communities have allowed the FIRE movement to really take hold in the past decade. Today, thousands of people across the world subscribe to podcasts, blogs and participate in discussion forums on how to live a parsimonious life."[94]

How much money would you need in order to do that? "Many (though not all) in the movement follow the 4% rule: by withdrawing just 4% of an investment, your income will consist mostly of interest and dividends, and you won't eat into the principal amount. The rule of thumb here is to save 25 times your required spending: for instance, for someone to draw £30,000 ($39,000) a year, they'd need £750,000 ($980,000)."

However, the BBC continues, "this rule has its flaws, especially when applied to young people. It's generally used for those retiring in their 60s, who aren't likely to need money for more than 30 years. The maths doesn't add up, says Holly Mackay, founder of consumer financial website Boring Money. 'If you retire in your 30s, you could be living for 70 more years. I think there's a bit of naivety.' Putting a precise dollar amount on the amount someone needs to retire at 35 is difficult, she says. If someone wants £20,000 a year, they'd need 55 times that – reduced assuming there were investments. 'But it's at least half a million, and then that only gets you £20,000 a year,' she explains. Using Mackay's rule of saving 55 times that amount, someone retiring at 35 would need £2.15 million ($2.75 million). Those calculations assume someone retiring at 35 won't work at all once they 'retire'. That's not the case for most in the FIRE movement."

You can go on and on playing with these somewhat theoretical numbers, but if you do that, I think you are missing the point of the FIRE idea. I agree with one case story in the BBC feature: "Despite the 'RE' (retire early) part of the FIRE movement moniker, the goal for Merz and Whiter isn't to quit their jobs at 27 or 43 and do nothing until they die. 'We're not meant to sit around and drink Mai Tais all day,' Merz says. 'Humans have an intrinsic need to work. We need to feel like a valued member of society, and that's not going to stop because you have an arbitrary number in the bank.' Rather, it gives them the flexibility to do what they want. Some choose to travel – on a budget, of course – while others simply pick and choose their work, rather than feeling trapped on the hamster wheel. 'I felt like I was beholden to the system,' says Whiter. 'I felt like I was in a prison camp, working to sustain a lifestyle I didn't actually want.' Now he's free. 'A lot of this stuff is emotional and psychological,' he says. 'You have to live through it to understand how powerful it is.'"

I couldn't agree more. This is not just about the money; it is about personal freedom, ultimately about leading a happy and purposeful life – and a more sustainable one as well.

Singapore is not really particularly known for its laid-back lifestyle. In my experience, the people here are some of the most focused, hard-studying, hard-working and ambitious you'll find anywhere. Even then, the local online daily had this feature out fairly recently, in March 2023: "Gen Zs and millennials may be the two youngest age groups currently in employment – but according to the OCBC Financial Index 2022, they are the ones who want to retire earlier than everyone else. While workers aged between 40 and 54, as well as between 55 and 65, preferred to retire at

61 and 65 years of age, respectively, millennials (aged 30 to 39) wanted to stop working at the age of 58, while Gen Z (aged 21 to 29) stated that 57 was their desired retirement age. A growing movement among millennials and Gen Z workers is the concept of FIRE (Financial Independence, Retire Early)."[95]

In all honesty, the story also highlighted that "the desire to retire early has been made more complicated by a range of environmental factors, such as an unbalanced post-pandemic recovery, high interest rates, inflation and market volatility. These have caused Singaporeans' financial wellness to decline, dipping one point from last year to match 2020's score of 61 out of a maximum of 100. The Index tracks each respondent's replies to 24 indicators across 10 pillars of financial wellness, including their saving habits and retirement planning. The Index also found that young Singaporeans were still keen on pursuing risky investments, such as cryptocurrencies, despite many experiencing losses in 2022's crypto crash. This could be due to the hope that cryptocurrency investments could make achieving FIRE possible."

The Singapore story even introduced two versions of the FIRE situation new to me: "Gen Z was also eyeing a more luxurious retirement, with 34 per cent – the highest proportion compared to other age groups – aiming for a retirement lifestyle that includes private healthcare, full-time domestic help and international holidays twice yearly. In FIRE terms, this is known as Fat FIRE – in which one enjoys an early retirement without having to cut back on life's luxuries."

In my humble view, that sort of defeats the purpose of the FIRE idea, to lead a simpler life, but then there is also another version:

The survey found that many young people would augment their regular day-job income with "gigs": "About 48 per cent of Gen Z were deriving side income from part-time endeavours, ranging from food delivery to running online businesses or giving tuition. Having a secondary stream of income can raise one's monthly earnings substantially. In addition, you can always carry on with your side hustle after quitting your day job – a form of FIRE known as Barista FIRE, where part-time or freelance work supplements income and helps workers keep one foot in the world of employment, should they need to return full-time."

OCBC bank concluded the report by saying: "When growing one's retirement funds, it's best to think long-term, seek professional advice and do research before investing. Young Singaporeans are generally good savers and with prudent financial habits, they can weather this storm – and eventually, achieve their financial goals and ideal retirement."

I would add that financial independence is absolutely possible to achieve; there is a lot of money sloshing around in our economy and return on capital is definitely possible – if you study how to achieve it and show a little patience. Going forward, many of the jobs available in our new economy might have lower productivity due to environmental constraints and competition from automation, and converting the financial capital into real stuff such as houses and cars has also been getting harder and harder, as we saw earlier.

On the positive side, for those who are lucky enough to be allowed to live in Singapore, here we have a relatively low tax on income. The first S$20,000 you make (after allowances) is tax-free, and the next S$10,000 is taxed at only 2%. You have to make over S$1 million to pay the top rate, 24% on what you make above that.[96] Considering the generous deductions and allowances available, most workers in Singapore do not pay any income tax at all; if your chargeable income (after reductions) is US$10,000 a month in Singapore, your monthly income tax bill would be US$870, quite reasonable for a developed country where personal income taxes provide less than a quarter of the government yearly revenue; the rest of government income is generated from corporate taxes, property taxes, sales taxes, fees and return on public investments. Overall, Singapore government expenditure as a percentage of GDP was 11.55% in 2021; the same year, it was 50.81% in my native Denmark, even higher at 59.04% in France, and 42.36% in the US, supposedly the land of the free.[97,98] Personally, it is difficult for me to see how you can call yourself a free and democratic country if you collect close to or more than half of the resources in the economy by force and redistribute them arbitrarily, with much of the value lost along the way in unproductive administrative bureaucracy. Living in a country with individual financial autonomy makes the FIRE journey so much easier.

RETIRE EARLY

That was the FI in FIRE, the financial independence. What about the RE, retire early? For that, I am with the "Barista FIRE" crowd. For many people, saving $2.75 million or even $1 million might be out of reach, so I recommend that you at least build up an "I quit" nest egg, take a break and decide what you really love to do, turn your passion into your work and supplement your savings and investment income with gig projects. I know lots of people who have done that. The nature community is full of such case stories: people who have left their professional careers early and perform lower-paid but much more satisfying tasks on a project basis. My wife is one of those. Retired from business, she now works in hornbill conservation, sometimes paid a bit, sometimes for free.

As we saw above, the BBC story calculated that you should save about $1 million before you can retire comfortably on your investment income alone. But we also saw that if you are able to cut some corners in your retirement, you don't need nearly that much. I suspect that some components of the new economy will work in your favour; others will work against you. Against you is the outlook for lower return on capital that I discussed in Chapter 5, mainly due to the fact that the debt culture has expanded the money supply to the point where a decent real (i.e. inflation-adjusted) return on investments going forward is difficult, maybe as low as an average of 1% p.a. That means that you will have to either beat the market (generate higher-than-average returns) or accumulate more funds. There are also observers such as the "peak prosperity" crowd who think that our collective economic pie is unlikely to grow much in the future, the way it has in the recent past, due to environmental and material constraints. And then there are researchers like Daniel Susskind who think that automation, AI, and technology in general, will soon make many jobs redundant, and lower the compensation available in others.

But here is the good news: We have generated so much wealth the last few decades that we really don't need that much more! Gen Y and Gen Z will not have to worry about taking care of their parents, the way many Baby Boomers and even Gen X did. Our parents were the Silent Generation (born 1928–45) and especially in developing countries, most of those old folks had a hard life, many had few savings. My wife and her siblings had to take care of their mother till she sadly passed away in 2016 – she had no means of her own to pay for housing and living expenses and healthcare. My sons, on the other hand, will not have to support me, nor my wife, ever. In fact, we might be able to help them out a bit – all the way to the end. Not all, but most Gen Y and Gen Z have parents who can help them on their way, with education, with a place to stay, and maybe with a bit of inheritance when the time comes.

The younger generations, when planning for their own retirement, will also find that they don't need much. Technology has made so many communication, entertainment and information options much cheaper. International telephone calls: Free. YouTube: Free. Google/Wikipedia: Free. Music: Almost free. I think a Spotify subscription is $10 per month or something like that, but that comes with unlimited downloads – my generation couldn't even buy one vinyl music album for that kind of money, and we bought a lot; after that came all the VHS tapes and the compact discs, now lying in landfills all over the world … imagine the money we wasted! In her house, my mother had a floor-to-ceiling shelf full of dictionaries, textbooks and encyclopaedias; during her time, that was the only way to store and access information. My son has all that data and more on the phone in his pocket. Most young people that I know today don't have a car; they don't need one and don't seem to care. The roads are full up anyway; public transport has improved tremendously most places in frequency, comfort and coverage; since people have increasingly concentrated into cities the last few decades, most young people today can walk or bicycle to the office or they simply work remotely from home.

The older generations, who participated in the Great Acceleration after 1950, have lots of material belongings to share: furniture, household items, collectibles and books. Eventually we will give it all away; it has no commercial value. Many people have so much stuff, they don't even know what to do with it. They can't keep it all at home, so they have to rent storage containers outside; globally, the so-called "self storage market" is worth $54 billion annually and expected to double within the next 10 years.[99] How silly and wasteful is that? Why don't we just stop making more things? We will have to simplify our lives, one way or another, when we run out of resources one day. I suggest we start now, before we are forced into it by circumstances.

Money alone cannot buy you happiness. The world is full of stories of obscenely rich people who end up committing suicide because they are not happy. However, not having enough money is miserable. So, the logical conclusion is that you have to get enough money to meet your needs, and then find another way to be happy. When I worked in industry, I stayed in some of the best hotels during business trips to Tokyo, Hong Kong and Manila. Now that I am retired, I have no desire to go back to that lifestyle – to be quite frank, I didn't even enjoy it that much at the time. Looking back over the years, as I mentioned in Chapter 1, some of my best memories have been staying in a tent in a remote place, off the trail, cooking instant noodles on a campfire, so that is what I want to do again. On my way there, into the wilderness, I prefer to stay with family and friends in a simple room.

HOW TO BE MISERABLE

One of my sons gave me a book recently: *How to Be Miserable: 40 strategies you already use* (Paterson, 2016). The title is of course meant ironically, but I enjoyed reading it. Randy Paterson is a Canadian psychologist and an expert in treating clinical depression. Based on his experience with patients, he identifies behaviour common to most of us that actually works to our disadvantage, such as focusing on the negative, eating and drinking too much, setting unrealistic goals, watching too much TV, spending too much money, insisting on perfection, being impulsive or intolerant, and keeping bad company – 40 little things we often do wrong, at one time or another.

Did I say "focusing on the negative"? But isn't that what I do frequently, when I warn about impending crises and misguided sustainability efforts? You could say that, I suppose; no one is perfect. But I take comfort in one of the Paterson's anti-lessons: "Become a toxic optimist". From his experience with over-optimistic people who end up in treatment for depression, Paterson warns that having unrealistic expectations about the future can lead to disappointment, and being unprepared for failure and setbacks in life can in turn lead to anxiety and mental breakdown. Paterson advises us to weigh probabilities of success and failure realistically and to have a Plan B to fall back on, in case the desired outcome doesn't materialize. I can sympathize with that strategy; it is a version of the good old mantra, "Hope for the best and prepare for the worst".

Philosophy professor David Benatar, author of *The Human Predicament: A Candid Guide to Life's Biggest Questions* (2017), says that "no matter how much evidence there is that the quality of human life is very bad, most humans will adhere to their optimistic views". He calls this the "optimism bias" and concludes: "The truth is simply too much for many people to bear. Even armed with various optimistic coping mechanisms, the quality of human life is not only much worse than most people think but actually quite awful." He sums up life this way: "Sandwiched between birth and death is a struggle for meaning, and a desperate attempt to ward off life's suffering." Right, Professor, this might be so, but what do you want us to do about it? Here is Benatar's reply: "I am recommending a response within the approximate terrain of pragmatic pessimism." In his view, this strategy "allows for *distractions* from reality, but not *denials* of it". For what it is worth, I tend to agree: Be a pragmatic pessimist!

NATURE: TO MANAGE, OR NOT TO MANAGE

So now that you have a strategy for coping with life's ups and downs, you can enjoy your RE, your early retirement, so much more. During this period, you can start focusing on what you love to do and what you are good at – those two are usually compatible. If you are alarmed about our sustainability, or lack of it, you can join the restoration movement. From the Great Acceleration, I postulated that we have moved into the Great Stagnation, and I now suspect we will move from there into the next phase, the Great Restoration.

This process has already begun; there are restoration and "re-wilding" projects going on all over the place. In fact, given a chance, nature will re-wild itself. Regarding this latter phenomenon, I can recommend *Islands of Abandonment: Life in the Post-Human Landscape* (2022) by Scottish journalist Cal Flyn. Flyn travels around the world and visits and describes natural places historically heavily scarred by human activity, but now, left on their own for decades, coming back from the dead. Some case stories such as Chernobyl in Ukraine and the dilapidated industrial areas of Detroit are fairly well known, but many others were new to me. All the places Flyn describes, however, have one thing in common: They show the powerful force of natural regeneration. Chernobyl and Detroit will never be really wild places again obviously, but Flyn points out how new forests are reclaiming abandoned farmland in Estonia and much of the rest of the former Soviet Union. In the news, we hear much about the shrinking rainforests in South America, West Africa and Southeast Asia, and I will be the last to belittle this catastrophic trend. But Flyn also points out that: "Currently, forests are declining in around a third of the world's countries, stable in a third, and growing in the final third." As an example, Flyn mentions the US, especially the east: "Agricultural land in the northeast US nosedived from 187,900 km² in 1880 to 48,800 km² in 1997, and as it did, the forest was quick to reclaim it. New England is the most thickly wooded region of America: from around 30 per cent cover then to over 80 per cent now. And with it, numbers of beaver and moose and white-tailed deer and bears and woodpeckers have rebounded too ... All in all, the American forest grew by around 360,000 hectares every year between 1910 and 1979."

Let me add two things to this. First of all, while some forests, such as deciduous temperate woodlands, can regrow quite well on their own, this is not the same for equatorial lowland rainforests.

Once a forest like that has been clear-felled, it will never come back, not in any meaningful timeframe. Tropical soil is inherently poor in nutrients, and once the topsoil with all the carbon and the fungi and the bacteria has been washed out from the exposed ground by the heavy rains, just the sandy minerals are left and only grasses and invasive creepers and shrubs will grow. Southeast Asia is full of these scarred landscapes. Secondly, if you want a healthy environment to come back anywhere, it will need help. As they say, once you break it, you own it. No matter what the conditions, a habitat that has been tampered with will always need management – forever!

The collapse of the cod industry in the North Sea is an often-mentioned case story of completely unsustainable production practices. All over the North Sea, cod was heavily overfished in the 1970s and into the 1980s; wonderful new technology like sonar and efficient trawling techniques meant that everything could be scooped out of the sea, not just the cod but also its smaller prey species of fish. Fish catches spiked, everyone was happy, what could possibly go wrong? Well, without prey left, the cod started feeding on its own young and a sudden and dramatic collapse occurred, especially so in the western Atlantic, on the Canadian side of the pond. In 1992, when cod catches were down to 1% of previous levels, the government had to step in and close the industry, fighting the fishermen all the way; over 30,000 people lost their jobs overnight. The situation was similar in the north-eastern Atlantic, off northern Norway. But here's the difference: While fisheries in Canada never really recovered, they did in Norway and nearby Iceland, which already in the 1970s fought several "cod wars" with the British, protecting, successfully as it turned out, their territorial waters against the greedy Anglo-Saxons. By leaving a little on the table for the fish to recuperate, the Nordic countries' cod fishery gradually recovered, today with strict scientific monitoring and fishing quotas. In Canada, UK and the EU countries that completely cleared the table, the fish never came back.

When I was a small kid in downtown Copenhagen, we had a fish shop down the street; I loved to tag along with my mother on her shopping trips and look at all the different fishes in tanks and on the counter. Fish was very cheap food then, so when my mother was short of money, which was most of the time, she would buy two or three kilos of herring or mackerel or cod for frying; they just cost a few kroners, and the fishmonger wrapped them with lighting speed in old newspapers – remember, there was no plastic then. Today herring is an expensive delicacy: 300 grams of marinated herring cost me S$10 or S$12. I am glad we are so much richer today; I can still afford to buy fish, at least a few grams of it!

THE CALL OF THE RE-WILDING

So my point is, the days are gone when we could just take freely from nature and then leave it to fend for itself. Like it or not, if you want to enjoy the benefits of a natural ecosystem, you first have to protect it from overexploitation and then you have to help what is left recover. You know the three "R"s of the green movement: Reduce, reuse and recycle. In that order of significance, in my personal view. But there are many others: Respect, React, Report, Respond, Resolve, Rebuild, Restore, and most importantly, Recover.

Regarding the recovery bit, Singapore has made itself into an international case story for successful re-wilding, but not by chance or by leaving nature on its own. We have a wetland reserve, the Sungei Buloh Wetland Reserve, established in 1993 and now an ASEAN Heritage Park, but the park is no wilderness. The abandoned prawn pond and mangrove areas require constant management of water levels and vegetation, coastal clean-up efforts, replanting and infrastructure development to regulate the flow of (human) visitors. I live near the 62-hectare Bishan Park and often go there for evening walks; here the upper reaches of the Kallang River were transformed back from a sterile concrete canal a few years ago to what is now a lush riverine habitat with various herons, some breeding in the tall trees along the stream. The shallow, winding and vegetated river is packed with fishes that attract otters. Today, Singapore might be the best place in the world to see the Smooth-coated Otter; this and many other of our animals are featured in countless impressive nature documentaries on Channel NewsAsia and the Discovery Channel, narrated by Sir David Attenborough himself.

When the British colonized Singapore in 1819, the island was almost entirely covered in lowland rainforest. But, according to a report by Singapore's NParks, "by 1900, 90% of the primeval forest had been cleared, mainly for agriculture". Today, "primary lowland dipterocarp forest and freshwater swamp forest cover only 0.28% and is confined to the Bukit Timah and Central Catchment Nature Reserves". And yet, amazingly: "Vegetation covers 56% of Singapore's total land area: 27% is actively managed (parks, gardens, lawns, etc.) and 29% is spontaneous vegetation".[100] So, Singapore is half-covered in greenery regrowth, some of it manicured, some of it less so. Along with the original forest, the Tiger and the Barking Deer and the Cream-coloured Giant Squirrel disappeared, as did 35 forest bird species pre-1940 and another 39 bird species since then; some of those have come back, most have not (Lim, 1992). But that man-managed habitat has nevertheless allowed some of the original animals to survive, while other invasive species have come in and filled up the niches now available to them.

As on-and-off active in the Nature Society (Singapore), I have been involved in some of the NGO-based re-wilding efforts taking place. You know, out there planting native trees in a denuded area of introduced shrubs, or fundraising for such campaigns. In the society, we always discuss among ourselves, as I suppose most do-gooders do, if we should take money for this from the people and the companies that caused the destruction in the first place. Are we helping them – the extractive forces – gain legitimacy that way? Are we condoning what they do by accepting their cash? Or should we just appreciate that they want to give some of their profits back for the restoration work? There is no easy answer to that, but like I mentioned with a financial ethical investment approach, we have an informal system of three categories of companies and donors that we are comfortable working with: the green, amber and red companies, with the amber category being oil companies and banks, and the red being people and organizations we just don't want to be associated with.

But one thing is certain: We do need help from businesses and wealthy individuals who have heard the call of the re-wilding and the nature conservation message. A friend of mine, Dr Pilai Poonswad, received the Rolex Award for Enterprise some years back for her work conserving hornbills in Thailand, and it helped her in her efforts to protect not just the birds, but the whole ecosystem they live in. With their Awards for Enterprise and Perpetual Planet Initiative, Rolex supports numerous scientific studies, conservation and re-wilding efforts around the globe. The Blue Planet Prize by the Asahi Glass Foundation supports researchers and organizations working on sustainability issues. Those are just a few examples that I know of; there are many other cases where businesses pay back and pay forward every year to fix the Earth. If you are qualified, take advantage of these opportunities to improve our conditions, or at least stop the rot here and there.

There are many indications that re-wilding meant to preserve local habitats and biodiversity can also serve a larger purpose. If you are concerned about climate change and global warming, you might take note of this study reported by the IUCN: "The findings show that these natural climate solutions are tremendously potent, providing an estimated 37% of cost-effective mitigation needed between now and 2030 to hold global warming below 2°C ... Of all ecosystems, forests have the greatest amounts of cost-effective mitigation opportunities to offer, making up about two-thirds of all nature-based climate solutions globally. Within the forest sector, reforestation offers the largest potential to mitigate climate change, followed by avoided deforestation and improved forest management ... Nature-based solutions can play a vital role in this regard in helping the global community, particularly in the near term, to achieve the longer-term objective of a decarbonised global economy."[101]

So there you have it. If you are concerned about environmental sustainability, please don't listen to the Occidental Petroleum

CEO and her extreme ideas of energy-intensive carbon capture and storage; just get out there and help plant some more trees!

And here is another thing to consider. The trees cannot rescue nature alone; we also need the animals that go with them. A paper co-authored by 15 scientists from eight countries found that animals are needed to "animate the carbon cycle": "Take wildebeests. They turn the Serengeti into a carbon sink by grazing, which reduces wildfire risk. Their waste, which contains carbon from the vegetation, is then buried in the soil by insects. In tundra, herds of musk oxen compact the snow, which keeps the soil frozen, therefore reducing methane emissions and increasing albedo – or the ability to reflect sunlight, which cools the local environment. Whales and other large ocean creatures take their embodied carbon to the bottom of the sea when they die. Other animals, like tapirs or elephants, engineer landscapes through their diet, which reduces plant competition, spreads seeds and enhances soil nutrition ... Yet the populations of animals in those habitats continue to be depleted by hunting."[102]

So, I suspect this will be our future: A constant, unpleasant, maybe somewhat antagonistic battle to preserve what little wilderness is left. And since this is unlikely to succeed, endless, but also somewhat more enjoyable, management and re-wilding undertakings that will keep the next generation of young people busy. They have to make do with what we, the Baby Boomers, left them. But as places like Singapore have shown, there are things that can be done to manage and improve nature. For that you need capital; as we have seen, financial capital generated by extracting from nature can be converted back into nature, if you have the will. And apart from that, re-wilding requires a well-functioning society with strong science, cooperative public institutions and a civic society to initiate and drive the change forward.

8

So, Are You ... Sustainable?

JUST A SHORT SUMMARY

In this book we have seen that a reduction in demand for resources, which the UN and a number of degrowth academics call for, is unlikely to happen. Nobody wants it. Not the politicians, not big business, not the rich, not the poor.

We also know that we will suffer devastating environmental impacts unless demand is reduced. So that means that devastating impacts are the most likely outcome.

The inevitable rise in global air and sea temperatures is just one problem. There are many others: biodiversity loss, resource scarcity, overpopulation, the financial debt burden, social discontent, wars between nations, environmental refugees ... all this is logically inevitable.

We can mitigate the consequences, but only up to a point. First of all we have to adapt. We have to batten down the hatches and make the best of it.

Obviously, our economic structure, capitalism, is incapable of incorporating degrowth. So since continuous growth in a confined space is a contradiction in terms, some have called for a radical change to our economic configuration, to capitalism itself. However, considering the popular benefits of the market mechanism, and the complete historical failure of socialism, I find that unlikely to come about.

I think the future of capitalism is already here. It looks like the free, and yet not-so-free, structure we have in a successful country like Singapore. Free because there is work for all, low taxes on income and plenty of opportunities to live the life you want. Not-so-free because this didn't come about by chance: economic incentives for FDI as well as hands-on management of labour market relations were crucial. Here the state provides support and financial subsidies for public housing, public health, public transport and education – virtually all the vital pillars of a prosperous society. There are even explicit social engineering policies in place to protect minorities and maintain ethnic harmony; there is zero tolerance regarding anything that could cause offence to anyone. And it has worked. If you don't believe me, read *Fifty Secrets of Singapore's Success* (Koh, 2020).

THE BIG PICTURE

So it seems to me that within the framework of such a societal structure, we have to make the best of our situation, what David Benatar calls "the human predicament". It is nice to assume that what you do yourself, in your daily choice of lifestyle, affects the bigger picture. I think that assumption is valid, but I also believe that your contribution – although important to you and your quality of life – is minuscule in the bigger scheme of things and unlikely to change the direction we are heading in. So don't get your hopes up.

As I mentioned before, my generation, the Baby Boomers, benefited tremendously from the Great Acceleration, the post-WWII economic expansion; so we have little reason to complain. But we have also experienced the cost, in terms of overpopulation and pollution, that went with all this prosperity. I visited the beaches off Kuantan and Terengganu on the Malaysian east coast for the first time in 1981, and the shores of Tioman Island and Bali, Indonesia, shortly afterwards. If anyone had told me then that I would one day visit again, and by then the previously pristine white sandy beaches would be muddy and grimy with sediments, the high-water mark covered in plastic, I wouldn't have believed them. How could you fill up a whole ocean with muck and plastic in just 40 years, a little more than one generation? Yet, that is exactly what happened.

Is there anything we can do about it? How can we stop the rot and reverse the trend? Frankly, I see lots of lofty statements but little that I personally believe will actually fly. The award-winning American journalist Elizabeth Kolbert asks the same question in her latest book, *Under a White Sky: Can we save the natural world in time?* (2022). Like me, she is struggling to find a positive reply to that question. She examines a number of case stories involving invasive species and coral restoration, and even explores geo-engineering options, such as putting reflective particles into the atmosphere to reduce sunlight penetrating to the Earth and thus global warming. If one line can sum up the book, it would be: "A future is coming where nature is no longer fully natural." It goes back to the re-wilding theme we considered in the previous chapter: The sick Earth requires management of the symptoms; but what about a cure?

There is recycling, right? A cornerstone in the sustainability approach, leading ideally to a circular economy. Well, here is a story about that on Singapore-based eco-business.com: "Just 8.6 per cent of the 100 billion tonnes of materials – including minerals, metals, fossil fuels and biomass – was put back into service in 2017, said a report by Amsterdam-based social enterprise Circle Economy, using the latest available data. That compares with 9.1 per cent of materials that were used again two years earlier, when annual consumption was 93 billion tonnes, CEO Harald Friedl told the Thomson Reuters Foundation. 'We are going from bad to worse in terms of circularity... We are risking global disaster if we continue this way of limitlessly using the world's resources.'"[103]

Lights, camera ... lots of meetings and statements ... but no action. In an article in *Nature* in 2022 by the who's who of degrowth experts, I find these suggestions:

- **Reduce less-necessary production** such as fossil fuels, mass-produced meat and dairy, fast fashion, advertising, cars and aviation.

- **Improve public services.** Universal public services can deliver strong social outcomes without high levels of resource use.

- **Introduce a green jobs guarantee,** such as installing renewables, insulating buildings, regenerating ecosystems and improving social care. It could be paired with a universal income policy.

- **Reduce working time.** This could be achieved by lowering the retirement age, encouraging part-time working or adopting a four-day working week.

- **Enable sustainable development.** This requires cancelling unfair and unpayable debts of low- and middle-income countries and curbing unequal exchange in international trade.

- **The "fiduciary duty" of company directors needs to be changed.** Instead of prioritizing the short-term financial interests of shareholders, companies should prioritize social and environmental benefits and take social and ecological costs into account.

- **Governments must stop subsidies for fossil fuel extraction.** They should tax ecologically damaging industries such as air travel and meat production.

Wealth taxes can also be used to increase public resources and reduce inequality.

- **Empirical research** is needed to shed light on the pros and cons of innovative monetary policy mechanisms.

- **Researchers need to study how provisioning systems link resource use with social outcomes.** No country currently meets the basic needs of its residents sustainably. Affluent economies use more than their fair share of resources, whereas lower-income countries are likely to need to use more.

- **Find alternative approaches to public housing** and a financial system that prioritizes housing as a basic need rather than as an opportunity for profit.[104]

We need to do this, we should do that. But can you start to sense one common theme in all these creative suggestions for research and new policies? Right, the distinguished authors admit that themselves towards the end of the op-ed: "Government action is crucial." Not a single one out of 10 items here is based on voluntary, democratic, market-based solutions. All this is just for armchair academics, conference hoppers and gabfest participants – the "Let's have another meeting next year" crowd. That is why I don't think that much of this will actually work.

We all wrestle with this contradiction: How much should the individual be expected to do, and how often do we need big government to step in? Regarding the environment, we need government to protect the commons and provide a framework for an orderly use of resources. We need a rule-based civilization to make sure corporations don't use child labour and dump their waste in the nearest lake. No society can tolerate illegal logging or mining or hunting; in those jurisdictions where public legislation and enforcement is weak, the environment suffers, and apart from a few criminals everyone is worse off. Look at the terrifying reports and images of beautiful tropical terrain devastated by illegal gold mining and animal poaching in Africa and South America. Even in supposedly enlightened Europe, countries facing the Mediterranean suffer from a cruel culture of illegal slaughter of songbirds and waterbirds that no one seems able to stop.

So personal freedom is a trade-off. Too much of it, and we end up in chaos and ecological collapse. Too little of it, and we end up in a dystopian Orwellian society with Big Brother watching us and telling us what to think and do. I don't have the answer to that dilemma. In general, I feel that solutions should come from the people, not top-down from government. So here are a few areas where I believe that big government is doing more harm than good and should really just step out of the way. For one thing, I agree with the degrowth academics that the state should stop subsidizing fossil fuels – that just doesn't make sense. I think they should also stop subsidizing electric vehicles – that doesn't make sense either. Stop giving money to fishermen killing more and more marine animals – unbelievably, global fishery subsidies amounted to $35.4 billion in 2018 alone.[105] Stop giving subsidized insurance to people suffering from natural disasters, the way the federal government does in the US, funding property flood insurance for rich house owners; the markets can never adjust to realistic values that way.[106] Stop subsidizing industrial agricul-ture – we have enough food, haven't you heard of the obesity epidemic? In the EU, the toxic Common Agricultural Policy has for decades unfairly robbed taxpayers and subsidized habitat destruction. Stop subsidizing children; let couples decided for themselves how many kids they want, but let those who want some pay the full price, wouldn't that be fair? By taking money from women who do the right thing by having fewer children and giving it to those who have many, you penalize the righteous and punish the environment. No, we *do not* need more young ones to take care of the old. That must be one of the most obvious fallacies of our time; a falsehood doesn't become the truth just because you repeat it endlessly. Increase interest rates and bank capital reserve requirements, balance the public budgets as well, so as to stop wrecking the Earth on debt. If you really must tax, tax consumption, not income, the way I explained that Singapore does.

LET'S LOOK AT THE FACTS

So, are you sustainable? Are we, as a civilization? No, sorry, I don't think so. Renaming ministries and hiring sustainability officers left and right doesn't make it so. The numbers and the facts count, and they just don't add up.

Take the much-touted energy transition. The message is that if we start installing a lot of solar panels and windmills and produce a lot of new electric vehicles, we can go on living like we always have, right? Not quite. As reported on RT News: "All those cars will need batteries, and all those batteries will need to be built with a small periodic table of minerals. And all those minerals need to be mined – in some cases strip-mining the rest of the planet's explored deposits ... It's estimated that 3 million more tons of copper will have to be mined per year to feed the production of 140 million EVs by 2030 – and that's copper, the most recycled metal on Earth. Nickel mining will have to increase by 1.3 million tons per year, and cobalt by 263,000 tons. Those are just batteries."[107]

We call this energy "renewable", but is it? Not according to the RT News report: "One big problem with going renewable all the way is that humans have not yet discovered a way to make any energy technology 100 percent renewable. Batteries we can currently make have a lifespan – a modern lithium battery, drained and recharged over and over, only maintains enough capacity to run an electric car for about 10 years. And those rare earth reserves are not infinite ... The problem is that the green future is still a vague, if beautiful, specter on the horizon – while the drill-scarred and salt-parched earth and polluted rivers are already a reality – one that will likely get worse as we feed the mineral-hungry renewables."

Even mainstream media outlet *Der Spiegel* from car-loving Germany has covered this dilemma: "There's a dirty secret hidden in every wind turbine. .... Each unit requires cement, sand, steel, zinc and aluminum. And tons of copper: for the generator, for the gearbox, for the transformer station and for the endless strands of cable. Around 67 tons of copper can be found in a medium-sized offshore turbine. To extract this amount of copper, miners have to move almost 50,000 tons of earth and rock, around five times the weight of the Eiffel Tower ... The bottom line: a lot of nature destroyed for a little bit of green power."[108]

This is the paradox behind the global energy transition. "Deposits in the poor South are being exploited so that the rich North can transition to environmental sustainability. At least to a lifestyle that appears sustainable."[109]

I agree with Mathis Wackernagel when he concludes in the *Der Spiegel* story: "Nature will continue to be depleted, in part because humanity hopes to live, work and travel in a more environmentally friendly manner in the future. For as long as we continue to maintain our current levels of prosperity, we will unavoidably continue to consume more resources, which is ultimately damaging to the biosphere. If we continue to use more than nature produces, we will exceed our planet's limits. It's like a bank account, says sustainability expert Wackernagel: You can overdraw your balance for a time, but not forever. Does that mean that renouncing consumption is the only solution to reducing our hunger for raw materials, as some have proposed? Wackernagel grimaces. 'That sounds to me like far too much individual suffering and sacrifice,' he says. A good life, he continues, is also possible within the ecological limits that exist. You don't need a two-ton electric vehicle to transport a person who weighs 75 kilograms. An electric bicycle can do the job just as well, he says."

This must be the bottom line: the data, the facts. Switching to "renewable" energy sounds good, but the case doesn't stack up. This type of development is simply not sustainable. That is all there is to it. A story on eco-business.com sums it up this way: "Global exploitation of natural resources – from water, sand and timber to oil, coal and gemstones – has more than tripled in 50 years, the United Nations said, warning of devastating environmental impacts unless demand is reduced. ... 'The Global Resources Outlook shows that we are ploughing through this planet's finite resources as if there is no tomorrow, causing climate change and biodiversity loss along the way,' said Joyce Msuya, acting head of UN Environment. 'Frankly, there will be no tomorrow for many people unless we stop.'"[110]

AND THE SMALL PICTURE

If you are disturbed by the state of our natural environment, if you are concerned for our sustainability going forward, ecologically, financially and eventually socially, don't just worry about it. Do something.

Each one of us is different. Some people are more apprehensive about our state of affairs than others; some are simply better informed and spend more time on these matters than others. It is a matter of priorities. I know people in both camps. Those who are truly troubled and think that this – sustainability – is a matter of life and death for humanity, an existential crisis. And those who are not worried at all, who believe that we will be alright, there is always more land over the horizon, the Earth has room for a whole lot more people, technology will save us, it always has, and by the way, global warming is a hoax.

I am not here to tell you what is right or wrong. But based on my experience, I am here to tell you that there are things you can do, depending on your level of concern. For the extremist, suffering from acute ecological anxiety, there is a group to join. It is called the Voluntary Human Extinction Movement. Seriously, there is such a thing. Professor Benatar, whom I mentioned before, is a declared antinatalist based on philosophical considerations; he and his sympathizers think it is immoral to procreate since human life has more bad than good. The voluntary extinction group is also against procreation but from an ecological stand-point: We people are the problem, and the Earth would be better off without us.

Les Knight is the founder of the voluntary extinction movement. "Our message is simple," he says. "We encourage people to stop procreating so the biosphere might return to its former glory, and everyone already here will be able to live life more abun-dantly." When he started his campaign in the 1990s, Knight says, "People from all over the world emailed me, saying they had thought they were alone. I got hate mail, too. 'You first,' is a common taunt. I don't know how many share my beliefs, but I speak to hundreds of advocates each year. We have active vol-unteers across the world, from India to Mexico." So how many kids should we have? Knight says: "Two is too many: computer models suggest even one-child families would result in 5–10 bil-lion people by 2100. Procreation today is the moral equivalent of selling berths on a sinking ship. It's true that society would be greatly diminished without children, but it isn't right to create them just because we like having them around. People worry that we won't have enough workers to support pensioners, but economic systems are artificial and can be adjusted. We don't need to breed more wage slaves to prop up an obsolete system. If we go extinct, other species will have a chance to recover. I'll never see the day when there are no humans on the planet, but I can imagine what a magnificent world it would be – provided we go soon enough."[111]

I don't know any human extinction proponents personally, but I do know people who choose not to have kids for moral, practical or financial reasons. If you really want to help the environment, many surveys show this is the best thing you can do: have fewer kids. A now-famous paper published in *Institute of Physics Science* in 2017 puts it this way: "We recommend four widely applicable high-impact (i.e. low emissions) actions with the potential to contribute to systemic change and substantially reduce annual personal emissions: having one fewer child (an average for developed countries of 58.6 tonnes CO_2-equivalent (tCO2e) emissions reduction per year), living car-free (2.4 tCO2e saved per year), avoiding airplane travel (1.6 tCO2e saved per roundtrip transatlantic flight), and eating a plant-based diet (0.8 tCO2e saved per year). These actions have much greater potential to reduce emissions than commonly promoted strategies like comprehensive recycling (four times less effective than a plant-based diet) or changing household lightbulbs (eight times less)."[112] So having one fewer child is by far the best thing you can do for the climate, and yet – so the authors lament – this is rarely discussed by government and big business who prefer to promote "lower-impact actions" like recycling and energy substitutions.

According to these experts, our environmental situation "records the aggregation of billions of individual decisions". I know someone here in Singapore who makes the individual decision not to drive. Right, many do that, you might say – except, this fellow doesn't take *any* form of road transport, not even public buses, so as not to support fossil fuel consumption; he prefers to walk all over the country for appointments and events. I also have a friend who doesn't use electric lights at home at night, and another who starves himself to minimize resource use.

And then, in the other corner of the ring you have the "We will prevail" camp. It goes like this: Malthus was wrong, and so was Paul Ehrlich; both warned about a "population bomb" (the title of Ehrlich's 1968 book) that never exploded. Fossil fuels and later industrialized farming, using plenty of artificial fertilizers and toxins, allowed us to grow the human population beyond all expectations. And there is room for a lot more. When horse manure became a problem in cities in the late 1800s, we just replaced the beasts with combustion engine cars. So now we will just replace all those with autonomous EVs and we will all be happy again. There is plenty of stuff left on Earth for this – and if that is not enough, we will get it from the oceans. And if that is still not enough, from the Moon. In the future, IT and AI will solve all our problems, future technological growth will generate untold riches for humanity, pay off all our debts – and if we still don't like it here, we can always escape through a wormhole or move to Mars.

For the rest of us, those in the middle of all this, we have to do the best we can. Even if you find either of these positions somewhat extreme, it doesn't hurt to examine your own lifestyle choices and check if there is room for improvement. Are you sustainable? I believe that the choice between a life of lavish excess and a life of complete austerity is false. You have to find your own way. I walk up the steps at home every day, even if I carry a few groceries. But I am the only one in the estate who does; years go by where I don't meet anyone on the steps, and there are only five storeys. I do the same thing at the MRT (the Singapore underground); the Marymount station that I often use has the longest, straightest staircase out of them all! Rarely, but occasionally, I will meet someone on the steps and I feel we have a kind of kinship.

Although you might feel sometimes that you are all alone out there, trying to save the Earth, you are not. There are some, not so many, but some, people out there like you. Find a network of likeminded activists that you want to support and engage with. Back to the famous three Rs: I have gone to some length here to express my scepticism about the Recycling bit. In most cases of material recycling, including lithium and plastic, that I have come across, the budget for energy, labour and capital use doesn't stack up. I have also made a strong case for simply Reducing instead, i.e. completely stopping the harmful extraction and throughput of resources and materials in the economy. Squeezed in between these two strategies is Reuse, and this approach shouldn't be dismissed outright. In fact, in my view this is where the individual in the small picture can really make a difference.

We have always had used-stuff shops. When I was a kid in the 1960s and early 1970s, I loved the outdoors and I would buy most of my gear from army surplus stores: clothes, parkas, boots, water canteens and that sort of thing. I did that because I couldn't afford new stuff, but I suppose the result was also beneficial to the environment. Now we have to do the same thing not because we have to, but out of choice, simply to conserve resources. Even today, most countries have army surplus shops; you don't have to spend thousands of dollars on over-priced designer outfits from Patagonia and The North Face to go for a hike in the woods.

My wife has started to explore clothes-swapping services. Like many middleclass ladies, she has several wardrobes full of pre-loved blouses and pants that she no longer wears. It turns out that there are quite a few clothes-exchange businesses operating in Singapore, and I am sure in most other countries as well. You just have to look for them a bit and make the effort of going there or dealing with them online. In other words: Reuse when you can, and reinvest the money you save this way for the rainy day – or the violent storm – that could be coming.

I am certain of one thing: If you want to be sustainable, have sustainable finances! That is why I devoted much of this book, and two of my previous ones, to financial independence and sustainability. Delay spending, accumulate a financial cushion and future-proof it the best you can. Max out your CPF Special Account, if you are lucky enough to have one of those. Americans can use their 401(k), but don't buy private insurance – those products don't work. For the rest of your cash, start with a conservative fixed deposit, then move into the securities market, stocks and bonds, when you understand the concepts. If you have the appetite for risk, and the time on your hands to deal with this, invest (a fraction of your net worth) in riskier alternative assets with higher potential for appreciation using financial derivatives.

I don't believe in life after death. But I do believe in money after life. While alive, Alfred Nobel, the Swedish explosive and weapons manufacturer, had a dubious reputation as the "merchant of death"; he facilitated the murder of thousands, maybe millions. But after he died, the money he made this way rehabilitated him, and today nice people in the Nordic establishment dress up and gather every year in his fond memory; the questionable way he generated his wealth is no longer discussed, only who will get his Nobel Peace Prize. Lots of wealthy people live on long after they are gone this way, through their foundations or buildings or institutions they founded and gave their name to. On a slightly smaller scale, I kept the money my mother left me in 2012. I still have it, I always will. Through investments in the Danish stock market, the portfolio has grown substantially; today I can use the dividends in her memory, to better the conditions for her grandchildren. If you want a life after death, set up a charitable foundation.

Notes

1   https://www.straitstimes.com/opinion/goh-chok-tongs-midnight-golf-game-with-us-president-bill-clinton-in-2000-the-untold-story

2   https://www.ceicdata.com/en/indicator/united-states/government-debt--of-nominal-gdp

3   https://pages.eiu.com/rs/753-RIQ-438/images/DI-final-version-report.pdf

4   https://tass.com/politics/1558207?utm_source=google.com&utm_medium=organic&utm_campaign=google.com&utm_referrer=google.com

5   https://www.todayonline.com/singapore/amid-russia-ukraine-war-small-countries-singapore-must-keep-sober-mind-and-look-beyond-headlines-shanmugam-2125676

6   https://www.statista.com/statistics/1293301/combined-defense-expenditures-nato/

7   https://www.nccs.gov.sg/singapores-climate-action/impact-of-climate-change-in-singapore/

8   http://www.wri.org/blog/2018/06/deforestation-accelerating-despite-mounting-efforts-protect-tropical-forests

9   https://www.youtube.com/watch?v=yExsEw6ZbGY

10 https://www.nytimes.com/2021/11/04/business/energy-environment/opec-russia-biden.html

11 https://www.theguardian.com/us-news/2023/mar/12/biden-oil-drilling-alaska-arctic-ocean-protection

12 https://www.bbc.com/news/science-environment-47203344

13 https://skeptics.stackexchange.com/questions/54293/does-global-warming-trap-as-much-heat-as-600-000-hiroshima-class-bombs-every-day

14 https://www.theatlantic.com/business/archive/2013/01/100-million-

worth-oil-money-richer-al-gore-doesnt-get-why-critics-are-being-so-critical/318926/

15 https://www.statista.com/statistics/1091926/atmospheric-concentration-of-co2-historic/

16 https://www.reuters.com/article/us-usa-fed-yellen-idUSKBN19I2I5

17 https://www.youtube.com/watch?v=REWeBzGuzCc

18 https://www.sg101.gov.sg/economy/digging-deeper-case-studies/1985

19 https://www.macrotrends.net/countries/WLD/world/poverty-rate

20 https://ourworldindata.org/from-1-90-to-2-15-a-day-the-updated-international-poverty-line

21 https://blogs.worldbank.org/developmenttalk/half-global-population-lives-less-us685-person-day

22 https://pittnews.com/article/5424/opinions/capitalism-the-worst-economic-system-except-for-all-the-others/

23 https://sustainabledevelopment.un.org/content/documents/5987our-common-future.pdf

24 https://www.formstack.com/blog/paper-statistics#:~:text=Worldwide%20consumption%20of%20paper%20has,being%20used%20for%20paper%20manufacturing.

25 https://www.crypto-news-flash.com/youtube-and-gold-mining-need-twice-as-much-energy-as-bitcoin-and-netflix-eth-pos-almost-free/

26 https://foreignpolicy.com/2018/09/12/why-growth-cant-be-green/amp/?__twitter_impression=true

27 https://yaleclimateconnections.org/2020/05/michael-moores-planet-of-the-humans-documentary-peddles-dangerous-climate-denial/

28 https://www.nature.com/articles/d41586-022-04412-x?utm_source=Nature+Briefing&utm_campaign=cc1890ce19-briefing-dy-20221216&utm_medium=email&utm_term=0_c9dfd39373-cc1890ce19-45420250

29 https://www.todayonline.com/singapore/economic-growth-competitiveness-important-lawrence-wong-2152586

30 https://www.investopedia.com/terms/u/uneconomic-growth

31 https://www.dst.dk/Site/Dst/Udgivelser/GetPubFile.aspx-
    ?id=19562&sid=landbruga

32 http://www.geografi-noter.dk/hf-geografi-landbrug.
    asp#:~:text=Siden%201950%20er%20landbrugets%20besk%C3%A6ft-
    igelse,samlede%20landbrugsareal%20er%20blevet%20ca.

33 https://www.dst.dk/da/Statistik/emner/oekonomi/
    betalingsbalance-og-udenrigshandel/import-og-eksport-af-var-
    er-og-tjenester#:~:text=Danmark%20eksporterer%20
    %C3%A5rligt%20varer%20og,handlen%20med%20varer%20og%20
    tjenester.

34 https://www.gatesnotes.com/The-Age-of-AI-Has-Begun

35 https://www.danielsusskind.com/media

36 https://www.bbc.com/news/technology-65102150

37 https://www.quora.com/What-is-the-meaning-of-never-memorize-
    something-that-you-can-look-up#:~:text=This%20quote%20was%20
    by%20Sir,available%20in%20books%20or%20sheets.

38 https://www.globalcitizen.org/en/content/jeff-bezos-space-flight-mon-
    ey-better-uses/#:~:text=Jeff%20Bezos%20just%20had%20his,alive%20
    spent%20around%20%245.5%20billion.

39 https://www.investopedia.com/ask/answers/042415/what-average-an-
    nual-return-sp-500.asp

40 https://journals.plos.org/plosone/article?id=10.1371/journal.
    pone.0144141

41 https://corpgov.law.harvard.edu/2022/11/17/exponential-ex-
    pectations-for-esg/#:~:text=In%20our%20base%20case%20
    scenario,industry%20as%20a%20whole').

42 https://www.bankrate.com/investing/esg-investing-statistics/

43 https://techwireasia.com/2022/08/greenwashing-is-becoming-a-big-
    problem-for-esg/

44 https://startuptalky.com/nestle-evil-company/

45 https://www.optimizedportfolio.com/gone-fishin-portfolio/

46 https://www.gic.com.sg/our-portfolio/

47 https://sybershel.com/peter-lim-billionaire-thanks-to-palm-oil/

48   https://www.straitstimes.com/world/regulate-cryptocurren-
cy-to-guard-against-money-laundering-davos-panel

49   https://jyllands-posten.dk/#ia10752983;finans

50   https://ycharts.com/companies/EQNR/dividend_yield

51   https://companiesmarketcap.com/oil-gas/largest-oil-and-gas-compa-
nies-by-market-cap/

52   https://www.eia.gov/outlooks/ieo/production/sub-topic-01.php

53   https://oilprice.com/Energy/Crude-Oil/The-Very-Real-Possibility-Of-
Peak-Oil-Supply.html

54   https://news.mongabay.com/2020/04/as-investment-giant-blackrock-
pulls-back-from-coal-ngos-urge-the-same-for-biomass-energy/

55   https://sponsored.bloomberg.com/article/axa/the-value-of-corporate-
governance-in-a-more-sustainable-world

56   https://newrepublic.com/article/165245/ikea-romania-europe-old-
growth-forest

57   https://www.channelnewsasia.com/business/apple-investigat-
ed-france-over-product-obsolescence-3490346

58   https://www.learnsignal.com/blog/hsbc-money-laundering/#:~:tex-
t=Evidence%20emerged%20that%20HSBC%20had,such%20as%20
Iran%20and%20Sudan.

59   https://www.bloomberg.com/news/articles/2022-02-17/corrup-
tion-bribery-probes-increase-at-standard-chartered#xj4y7vzkg

60   https://www.bbc.com/news/world-europe-45167906

61   https://www.brainyquote.com/quotes/dick_cheney_564190

62   https://www.bbc.com/news/world-europe-65485908

63   https://coinmarketcap.com/

64   https://companiesmarketcap.com/gold/marketcap/#:~:text=Esti-
mated%20Market%20Cap%3A%20%2413.472%20T,is%20currently%20
arround%20%2413.472%20T.

65   https://www.statista.com/statistics/270126/largest-stock-ex-
change-operators-by-market-capitalization-of-listed-companies/

66   https://www.currentmarketvaluation.com/models/price-earnings.php

67 https://www.straitstimes.com/singapore/environment/hundreds-turn-up-in-red-at-hong-lim-park-for-first-singapore-climate-rally

68 https://www.channelnewsasia.com/sport/f1-singapore-grand-prix-records-highest-attendance-races-13-year-history-2980631

69 https://www.imf.org/en/Publications/WEO/Issues/2023/01/31/world-economic-outlook-update-january-2023

70 https://www.visualcapitalist.com/worlds-poorest-countries-2023-gdp-per-capita/

71 https://ourworldindata.org/

72 https://www.bloomberg.com/news/audio/2022-10-26/oxy-ceo-hollub-pitches-net-zero-oil-do-you-buy-it-podcast

73 https://www.bloomberg.com/news/videos/2023-02-06/occidental-ceo-share-repurchases-are-a-priority

74 https://polb.com/port-info/news-and-press/singapore-long-beach-l-a-ports-to-establish-green-digital-shipping-corridor-11-07-2022/

75 https://www.edb.gov.sg/en/business-insights/insights/singapore-to-have-world-s-largest-sustainable-aviation-fuel-plant.html

76 https://www.statista.com/statistics/655057/fuel-consumption-of-airlines-worldwide/#:~:text=The%20global%20fuel%20consumption%20by,57%20billion%20gallons%20in%202021.

77 https://www.airbus.com/en/sustainability/respecting-the-planet/decarbonisation/sustainable-aviation-fuel#:~:text=A%20key%20driver%20for%20achieving,than%201%25%20of%20operated%20flights.

78 https://theicct.org/publication/global-aviation-icao-net-zero-goal-jan23/#:~:text=In%20October%202022%2C%20member%20states,emissions%20from%20aviation%20by%202050.

79 https://www.bbc.com/news/science-environment-65727664

80 https://www.bbc.com/news/science-environment-61556984

81 https://www.youtube.com/watch?v=fv9HQtXBTo4

82 https://rock.geosociety.org/net/gsatoday/archive/22/12/article/i1052-5173-22-12-4.htm#:~:text=The%20expansion%20of%20infrastructure%20and,of%20agricultural%20land%2C%20is%20unsustainable.

83 https://www.bbcearth.com/news/when-dinosaurs-roamed-antarctica

84 https://www.sciencedaily.com/releases/2013/09/130924153956.
htm#:~:text=%22In%20our%20study%2C%20we%20found,bal-
ance%20with%20the%20higher%20levels.%22

85 https://www.brainyquote.com/quotes/joseph_de_maistre_138331

86 https://edition.cnn.com/2023/02/05/energy/
single-use-plastics-volume-grows-climate-intl-hnk?fbclid=IwAR3YTc-
CkUemIx39QjqMEws9QiMR-xD-3wSzorIw46bBvWPjNTi4HcdBMePQ

87 http://www.eco-business.com/news/will-sustainability-ev-
er-trump-price-for-asian-consumers/

88 https://www.bbc.com/news/business-64714107

89 http://demographia.com/db-intlcitylossr.htm

90 https://www.todayonline.com/world/japan-has-millions-empty-hous-
es-want-buy-one-s33000-2153446

91 https://www.rainforest-rescue.org/petitions/1182/electric-vehi-
cles-are-stealth-rainforest-killers?t=362

92 https://www.iea.org/commentaries/global-suv-sales-set-another-re-
cord-in-2021-setting-back-efforts-to-reduce-emissions

93 https://jyllands-posten.dk/nyviden/ECE10829389/international-
gruppe-laeger-vi-goer-alt-for-mange-til-syge/

94 https://www.bbc.com/worklife/article/20181101-fire-the-movement-
to-live-frugally-and-retire-decades-early

95 https://www.todayonline.com/brand-spotlight/achieve-fire-dont-rely-
spark-speculation-2116146

96 https://www.iras.gov.sg/taxes/individual-income-tax/
basics-of-individual-income-tax/tax-residency-and-tax-rates/individu-
al-income-tax-rates

97 https://www.imf.org/external/datamapper/exp@FPP/USA/FRA/JPN/
GBR/SWE/ESP/ITA/ZAF/IND

98 https://www.theglobaleconomy.com/Singapore/government_size/#:~:-
text=The%20average%20value%20for%20Singapore,154%20
countries%20is%2016.83%20percent.

99 https://storeganise.com/blog/self-storage-trends#:~:text=This%20

is%20exemplified%20by%20the,market%20experiences%20the%20
demand%20pull.

100 https://www.nparks.gov.sg/sbg/research/publications/gardens-bulletin-singapore/-/media/sbg/gardens-bulletin/
gbs_63_01,-a-,02_y2011_v63_01,-a-,02/63_01,-a-,02_205_y2011_v63p1,-a-,p2_gbs_pg_205.pdf

101 https://www.iucn.org/news/climate-change/201812/protecting-climate-protecting-nature

102 https://www.washingtonpost.com/business/energy/2023/04/11/
rewilding-nature-is-no-solution-if-all-you-ve-got-are-trees/a30e23d8-d821-11ed-aebd-3fd2ac4c460a_story.html

103 https://www.eco-business.com/news/world-risks-disaster-as-reuse-of-natural-resources-declines/

104 https://www.nature.com/articles/d41586-022-04412-x?utm_
source=Nature+Briefing&utm_campaign=cc1890ce19-briefing-dy-20221216&utm_medium=email&utm_term=0_c9dfd39373-cc1890ce19-45420250

105 https://www.sciencedirect.com/science/article/pii/
S0308597X19303677

106 https://www.politico.com/agenda/story/2017/08/08/hidden-subsidy-rich-flood-insurance-000495/

107 https://www.rt.com/news/466028-clean-energy-fuels-dirty-mining/

108 https://www.spiegel.de/international/world/
mining-the-planet-to-death-the-dirty-truth-about-clean-technologies-a-696d7adf-35db-4844-80be-dbd1ab698fa3

109 https://www.spiegel.de/international/world/
mining-the-planet-to-death-the-dirty-truth-about-clean-technologies-a-696d7adf-35db-4844-80be-dbd1ab698fa3

110 https://www.eco-business.com/news/no-tomorrow-for-many-unless-consumption-fallsun/

111 https://www.theguardian.com/lifeandstyle/2020/jan/10/i-campaign-for-the-extinction-of-the-human-race-les-knight

112 https://iopscience.iop.org/article/10.1088/1748-9326/aa7541

References

Angus, Ian. 2016. *Facing the Anthropocene: Fossil capitalism and the crisis of the Earth system.* New York: Monthly Review Press.

Baker, Kent, Holzhauer, Hunter and John R. Nofsinger. 2022. *Sustainable Investing: What Everyone Needs to Know.* New York: Oxford University Press.

Benatar, David. 2017. *The Human Predicament: A Guide to Life's Biggest Questions.* New York: Oxford University Press.

Dietz, Rob and Dan O'Neill. 2013. *Enough is Enough: Building a Sustainable Economy in a World of Finite Resources.* San Francisco: Berrett-Koehler Publishers.

Donnelly, Seth. 2019. *The Lie of Global Prosperity: How Neoliberals Distort Data to Mask Poverty and Exploitation.* New York: Monthly Review Press.

Ebrey, Patricia. 2010. *The Cambridge Illustrated History of China: Second Edition.* New York: Cambridge University Press.

Flyn, Cal. 2022. *Islands of Abandonment: Life in the Post-Human Landscape.* London: William Collins.

Heinberg, Richard. 2011. *The End of Growth: Adapting to Our New Economic Reality.* Canada: New Society Publishers.

Hickel, Jason. 2018. *The Divide: A Brief Guide to Global Inequality and its Solutions.* London: Windmill Books.

Hickel, Jason. 2020. *Less is More: How Degrowth Will Save the World.* London: Windmill Books.

Jackson, Tim. 2009. *Prosperity without Growth: Economics for a Finite Planet.* New York: Earthscan

Jackson, Tim. 2021. *Post Growth: Life after Capitalism.* Cambridge: Polity Press.

Klare, Michael T. 2013. *The race for what's left: the global scramble for the world's last resources.* New York: Metropolitan Books.

Klein, Naomi. 2014. *This Changes Everything: Capitalism vs. The Climate.* London: Penguin Books.

Ko, David and Richard Busellato. 2021. *The Unsustainable Truth: How Investing for the Future is Destroying the Planet and What to Do About It.* UK: Panoma Press.

Koh, Tommy (edited). 2020. *Fifty secrets of Singapore's success.* Singapore: Straits Times Press.

Kolbert, Elizabeth. 2022. *Under a White Sky: Can we save the natural world in time?* Dublin: Penguin Random House.

Lim, Kim S. 1992. *Vanishing Birds of Singapore.* Singapore: The nature Society (S).

Martenson, Chris and Adam Taggart. 2015. *Prosper! How to Prepare for the Future and Create a World Worth Inheriting.* Arizona: Peak Prosperity Books.

Paterson, Randy. 2016. *How to Be Miserable: 40 strategies you already use.* California: New Harbinger Publications.

Plimer, Ian. 2014. *Not for Greens.* Australia: Connor Court Publishing.

Quammen, David. 2013. *Spillover: Animal Infections and the Next Human Pandemic.* New York: W.W. Norton & Company.

Rickards, James. 2017. *The Death of Money: The coming collapse of the international monetary system.* New York: Penguin Random House.

Rickards, James. 2019. *Aftermath: Seven secrets of wealth preservation in the coming chaos.* New York: Portfolio Penguin.

Rogers, Chris. 2014. *Capitalism and its Alternatives.* London: Zed Books.

Rothstein, Adam. 2017. *The End of Money: The story of bitcoin, cryptocurrencies and the blockchain revolution.* London: John Murray Learning.

Roubini, Nouriel. 2022. *Megathreats: The ten trends that imperil our future, and how to survive them.* London: John Murray (Publishers).

Smith, Stephen. 2011. *Environmental Economics: A Very Short Introduction.* New York: Oxford University Press.

Strange, Morten. 2016. *Be Financially Free: How to become salary independent in today's economy.* Singapore: Marshall Cavendish.

Strange, Morten. 2018. *The Ethical Investor's Handbook: How to grow your money without wrecking the earth.* Singapore: Marshall Cavendish.

Susskind, Daniel. 2021. *A World Without Work: Technology, Automation and How We Should Respond.* Dublin: Penguin Books.

Swedroe, Larry and Samuel C. Adams. 2022. *Your Essential Guide to Sustainable Investing: How to Live Your Values and Achieve Your Financial Goals with ESG, SRI, and Impact Investing.* UK: Harriman House.

The Economist. 2021. *Pocket World in Figures.* London: Profile Books.

Wagner, Gernot and Martin L. Weitzman. 2015. *Climate Shock: The economic consequences of a hotter planet.* New Jersey: Princeton University Press.

Wallace-Wells, David. 2020. *The Uninhabitable Earth: Life After Warming.* New York: Tim Duggan Books.

About the Author

Morten Strange is a Danish-born, Singapore-based independent financial analyst with a deep interest in sustainability issues. He is the author of *Be Financially Free: How to Become Salary Independent in Today's Economy* (2016) and *The Ethical Investor's Handbook: How to Grow Your Money Without Wrecking the Earth* (2018). His commentaries and interviews have appeared in the *Straits Times*, Today Online and international media. Since retiring at the age of 33, he has pursued his interests in economics, writing, photography and environmental conservation.